Architectural Design
September/October 2008

New Urban China

Guest-edited by Laurence Liauw

IN THIS ISSUE

Main Section

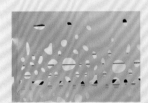

WILEY
wiley.com

Architectural Design

Vol 78 No 5
ISBN 978-0470 75122 0

C O N T E N T S

Editorial Offices
John Wiley & Sons
International House
Ealing Broadway Centre
London W5 5DB

T: +44 (0)20 8326 3800

Editor
Helen Castle

Regular columnists: Valentina Croci, David Littlefield, Jayne Merkel, Will McLean, Neil Spiller, Michael Weinstock and Ken Yeang

Freelance Managing Editor
Caroline Ellerby

Production Editor
Elizabeth Gongde

Design and Prepress
Artmedia Press, London

Printed in Italy by Conti Tipocolor

Sponsorship/advertising
Faith Pidduck/Wayne Frost
T: +44 (0)1243 770254
E: fpidduck@wiley.co.uk

Front cover: Montage by Laurence Liauw. Image © Laurent Gutierrez + Valerie Portefaix

Editorial Board

Subscribe to ΔD

ΔD is published bimonthly and is available to purchase on both a subscription basis and as individual volumes at the following prices.

PRICES
Individual copies: £22.99/$45.00
Mailing fees may apply

ANNUAL SUBSCRIPTION RATES
Student: UK£70/US$110 print only
Individual: UK £110/US$170 print only
Institutional: UK£180/US$335 print or online
Institutional: UK£198/US$369 combined print and online

Subscription Offices UK
John Wiley & Sons Ltd
Journals Administration Department
1 Oldlands Way, Bognor Regis
West Sussex, PO22 9SA
T: +44 (0)1243 843272
F: +44 (0)1243 843232
E: cs-journals@wiley.co.uk

[ISSN: 0003-8504]

Prices are for six issues and include postage and handling charges. Periodicals postage paid at Jamaica, NY 11431. Air freight and mailing in the USA by Publications Expediting Services Inc, 200 Meacham Avenue, Elmont, NY 11003.
Individual rate subscriptions must be paid by personal cheque or credit card. Individual rate subscriptions may not be resold or used as library copies.

All prices are subject to change without notice.

Postmaster
Send address changes to 3 Publications Expediting Services, 200 Meacham Avenue, Elmont, NY 11003

RIGHTS AND PERMISSIONS
Requests to the Publisher should be addressed to:
Permissions Department
John Wiley & Sons Ltd
The Atrium
Southern Gate
Chichester
West Sussex PO19 8SQ
England

F: +44 (0)1243 770620
E: permreq@wiley.co.uk

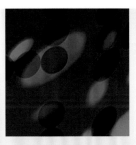

AD+

Editorial

Helen Castle

Every title of *AD* brings with it new discoveries and revelations. However, never has a single issue shifted my worldview and perceptions so much. China's geography and demographics alone require a different mindset. China may have a slightly smaller landmass than the US (3.7 million to its 3.8 million square miles), but the US's population is diminutive when compared to that of China: China has over a third more people. For those of us who have lived most of our lives on an overcrowded northern European island, the scale of China is difficult to grasp. It is, however, the rate and intensity of urban change in China over the last three decades that make it truly unprecedented. At a time when a 15-hectare (38-acre) site, like that at Battersea Power Station, has proved a stumbling block for developers in London, 95 per cent of Beijing's buildings have been razed and replaced.[1] Speed and size of construction alone are awe-inspiring, bringing with them unique opportunities to build. These are not just the much-publicised flagship icons by foreign architects such as Herzog & de Meuron's 'Bird's Nest' Olympic Stadium and Rem Koolhaas' CCTV Tower in

Beijing, or the great swathes of standardised mega-city housing blocks that are being constructed across the country; there is a new talented generation of indigenous architects emerging who, having been educated at top institutions overseas, are now determined to build innovatively at home (see pp 82–93). Such unprecedented urban expansion inevitably guzzles resources and it is this that makes extensive construction a global concern, with China buying up natural minerals, building materials and fuels around the world. It also presents a challenge to the international status quo, and anticipates a future with China having a far greater influence on the world politically and economically, whether it is the mode in which cities and buildings are produced or the source of their investment.

The velocity of change in China is such that, as this issue closes, it is very apparent that recent events could well shift the pattern and momentum of urban development. Construction has been matched by devastation: the May 2008 earthquake in Sichuan Province left thousands dead and homeless and has required the government to focus on the building of new infrastructure and housing in affected areas. More than anything, though, the continuing rate of urbanisation in China rests on a burgeoning economy. With the onset of the credit crunch in the US, and widespread talk of recession in the West, is China's exponential growth sustainable? Is it not conceivable that the factory of the world will be affected by the economic downturn elsewhere? I put this question to Joe Studwell, author and ex-Editor of *China Economic Quarterly*. His belief is that to some extent China will be supported by its extensive internal market: 'China's net exports can fall quite a lot without a major impact on overall growth,' but that demographics and labour supply will be key to longer-term growth.[2] Li

China simultaneously grapples with the enormity of destruction and construction. Here (top image) survivors of the earthquake that hit Qingchuan county in Sichuan Province in May 2008 search for their belongings in the debris of their collapsed homes. A Chinese migrant worker (bottom image) walks past Skidmore, Owings & Merrill's China World Trade Center Tower 3 under construction, just before the start of the 2008 Beijing Olympic Games.

Jin and Shan Li, writing in *The Wall Street Journal Asia*, have also emphasised that 'China's core competence lies not in its technological or managerial superiority, but rather in its abundant and cheap labor', the threat to its competitive advantage lying ostensibly in a 'rapid appreciation of the yuan' combined 'with a weak U.S. economy'. Increases in pay could lead to the failure of labour-intensive businesses, significantly disrupting 'the ongoing process of urbanization and industrialization of the Chinese economy'.[3] At present, economic forecasts for China issued by the likes of the Economist Intelligence Unit remain broadly positive: 'Real GDP growth is forecast to slow but will remain impressive, easing from 11.9% in 2007 to 8.6% in 2012.'[4] There is no doubt forthcoming vicissitudes in the economic climate could have a significant impact on the speed and rate of construction. However, what this title – so effectively guest-edited by Laurence Liauw – allows you to do is to realise the full magnitude of urban change in the last three decades, and its transformative effects on both China and the rest of the world. Δ

Notes
1. Isabel Hilton, 'First City of the Future', *Observer* (Review Beijing Special Issue), 6 July 2008, p 5.
2. Joe Studwell, email to Helen Castle 17 June 2008.
3. Li Jin and Shan Li, *The Wall Street Journal Asia*, 3 July 2008. http://online.wsj.com/article/SB121503329669924121.html?mod=googlene ws_wsj.
4. Country Data, from the Economist Intelligence Unit, 3 July 2008: www.economist.com/countries/China/profile.cfm?folder=Profile%2DEconomi c%20Data.

Introduction

'Leaping Forward, Getting Rich Gloriously, and Letting a Hundred Cities Bloom'[1]

By Laurence Liauw

The urbanisation of the Pearl River Delta (the fastest in China) has been driven primarily by the development of mono-type 'factory towns' catering for products 'Made in China'. These factory towns house mainly migrant workers, and follow a repetitive pattern of self-organised urban development and generic buildings.

China's rapid urbanisation is mirrored by Shenzhen city's genesis and growth around the border area (with Hong Kong) of Lowu, a group of fishing villages of little more than 30,000 people in the late 1970s to today's population of more than 12 million.

Deng Xiaoping, the late leader of the Communist Party of China, during his landmark visit to Shenzhen SEZ in 1982. Here he is shown with other officials inspecting the new masterplan for Shenzhen that was to trigger rapid urbanisation for the next seven years.

Full Speed Ahead in the South

This year marks the thirtieth anniversary of market-oriented economic reform in China, which has resulted in urbanisation on a massive scale: the urbanisation rate rising from 20 per cent in 1980 to currently over 44 per cent, with more than 400 million people moving to cities from rural areas.[2] The process was kick-started in 1978 by Deng Xiaoping's Open Door Policy, which committed China to adopting policies that promoted foreign trade and economic investment. It was launched during his first tour of Southern China, and resulted in five Special Economic Zones (SEZs) being established between 1980 and 1984 at: Shantou, Shenzhen and Zhuhai in the coastal region of Guangdong Province; Xiamen on the coast in Fujian Province; and the entire island province of Hainan. These SEZ cities in the Pearl River Delta (PRD) have become arguably China's greatest contemporary urban invention, achieving rapid economic growth with GDP of over 13 per cent per annum since 1996.[3]

The booming transformation of cities has totally reconfigured the nation's metropolises and the urban life of its people. Shenzhen, which is on the Southern China coast adjacent to Hong Kong, was the prototype SEZ. It acted as an urban laboratory, far enough from Beijing to either succeed or fail. A tabula rasa, it grew from scratch; a mere group of fishing villages of 30,000 people in the late 1970s, its population has increased 400-fold since the 1980s.[4] The chaotic urbanisation of the PRD, Southern China's factory belt, was first introduced to Western audiences as a cluster of 'cities of exacerbated differences' (COEDs) by Rem Koolhaas in his 2001 book *Great Leap Forward*,[5] which was based on fieldwork undertaken with Harvard Graduate School of Design students in 1996 (see pp 60–3, Zhi Wenjun and Liu Yuyang, 'Post-Event Cities'; and pp 98–81, Doreen Heng Liu, 'After the Pearl River Delta: Exporting the PRD – A View from the Ground'). The PRD has since become a role model for major regional developments elsewhere in China, most notably areas such as the Yangtze River Delta around Shanghai and the Bohai Bay region around Beijing and Tianjin.

This euphoria for industry-driven urbanisation has recently spilled over into countries outside China, such as India, Africa, Vietnam and Russia (see pp 74–7, Laurence Liauw, 'Exporting China'). Certain political road bumps such as the 1989 student protests tempered China's march for economic reform and urbanisation, but Deng again ignited another sustained construction boom with his second tour of Southern China in 1992, coupled this time with sweeping changes in land reforms and a budding real-estate market (see pp 22–5 and pp 32–5, Sun Shiwen, 'The Institutional and Political Background to Chinese Urbanisation', and Zhang Jie, 'Urbanisation in China in the Age of Reform').

With the growth of urban wealth, 'Made in China for export' has become 'Made in China from elsewhere', with products being produced abroad for domestic consumption in China, especially in terms of the production of urban space, assemblage of raw materials and consumption of energy (see pp 72–3, Kyong Park, 'The End of Capitalist Utopia?'). The scale and speed of new urban China's construction boom has been widely documented in terms of its spectacular magnitude and architectural variety – according to the Ministry of Construction, China plans to build 2 billion square metres (21.5 billion square feet) each year (half that of the world total), is already using up to 26 per cent of the world's crude steel and 47 per cent of its cement,[6] and will have built 80 billion square metres (861.1 square feet) of new housing by 2010.[7] Jiang Jun's general taxonomy of city types (see pp 16–21, Jiang Jun and Kuang Xiaoming, 'The Taxonomy of Contemporary Chinese Cities (We Make Cities: A Sampling') reveals the sociocultural side effects of urbanisation on various sectors of Chinese society and the type of urban processes that actually determine the physical manifestation of the majority of cities.

'Destroy the Old to Establish the New'

Chairman Mao's famous political slogan of 1966 during the Cultural Revolution, urging China to rapidly industrialise, with somewhat disastrous consequences such as widespread famine, is now being re-enacted literally in a very different guise in this era of market reforms that has spawned hundreds of new Chinese cities. Since 1998, another revolution has been taking place in which new 'commodified' private housing for the masses has been replacing state-subsidised housing provided by work units, paralleled in commercial sectors by the decline in state-owned industries and the rise of privately owned manufacturing. Since the early 1990s, sweeping economic and land reforms have triggered one of the biggest real-estate booms in history: according to recent surveys by the Sohu.com website, real estate has become the most profitable industry in China with more than RMB2.5 trillion currently invested. Cities already account for 75 per cent of China's GDP and this is expected rise to 90 per cent by 2025[8] (see also pp 20–5, Sun Shiwen, and pp 26–31, Huang Weiwen, 'Urbanisation in Contemporary China Observed: Dramatic Changes and Disruptions'), determining much of the new physical appearance of China's major cities with both generic and spectacular architecture. Typically architecture is produced either via direct commissions for standard generic buildings or through international design competitions for iconic buildings.

Compared to the newly built commerce- and manufacturing-based towns, mature historical cities that have an older urban fabric are not faring so well. They are rapidly being destroyed on a large scale to make way for new developments. This erasure of entire sections of cities such as Beijing, where varying reports of anything between 300,000 and 1.5 million people have been displaced for the 2008 Olympics,[9] and Shanghai in preparation for mega-events (see pp 60–3, Zhi Wenjun and Liu Yuyang) is also driven by profitable generic developments yielding tax income to the authorities (see pp 22–5, Sun Shiwen). Mckinsey Global Institute estimates that over the past decade land sales have contributed to more than 60 per cent of some Chinese cities' annual income.[10] Rocketing land prices have prompted urban renewal and the destruction of the vernacular building fabric, which is often several hundreds of years old, while also causing the mass displacement of established communities from their natural habitats to new suburban areas. The effects of this brutal displacement have been compounded by eviction and insufficient compensation, triggering much social unrest, as witnessed typically by the persistent existence of 'nail houses' on demolition sites where occupiers are resisting relocation (see pp 44–7, Wang Jun, 'The "People's City"'). Destruction of old communities and a tight-knit urban fabric call into question the nature and effectiveness of the newly created public spaces that have replaced traditional streets in Chinese cities, raising the question as to their long-term contribution to People's Cities (see pp 48–51, Shi Jian, 'Street Life and the "People's City"').

Chairman Mao's famous 1966 slogan 'Destroy the old to establish the new' is being re-enacted literally in a different guise as entire historic neighbourhoods (such as Pudong, shown here) are totally erased to be replaced by new commercial developments. Slow infrastructure development means that citizens often have to walk to work through wastelands and construction sites.

The rapid transformation of major cities such as Shanghai (top image) means the vernacular building fabric coexists alongside new generic globalised towers in a seemingly chaotic agglomeration. In Beijing (bottom image), many *hutongs* (narrow lanes lined with traditional courtyard houses) have been demolished for redevelopment, displacing local communities ahead of the Olympics and the vision of a 'New Beijing'.

Destruction of old communities and a tight-knit urban fabric call into question the nature and effectiveness of the newly created public spaces that have replaced traditional streets in Chinese cities, raising the question as to their long-term contribution to People's Cities.

Urban villages (previously farmland) spring up within cities as high-density settlements that attract migrant workers. In 2005 the local authorities demolished one of Shenzhen's 192 urban villages (shown here). Social displacement remains a serious challenge for society, as witnessed during the 2008 snowstorms that created huge bottlenecks of migrant workers returning home for the spring festival at many train stations (such as in Guangzhou, shown here).

Many major cities now have impressive urban-planning exhibition centres showing huge-scale models of the entire city. Their ambition and surreal quality is matched only by the constantly changing 'real' model outside, which sometimes resembles a dystopian vision of instant urbanisation on steroids. Thus the reality of city development often changes faster than the show model can be adjusted.

'Capitalism with Chinese Characteristics' and the 'New Socialist Village'

Market-oriented economics under communist rule is commonly referred to by politicians and economists as 'Capitalism with Chinese characteristics'. This paradoxical model of the Planned Economy has largely been responsible for instigating the mass migration of villagers to cities and towns seeking work and higher wages. A 'floating population' of up to 150 million migrant workers[11] is now moving around China without gaining *hukou* (household resident) status in the cities that they live in (see pp 26–31, Huang Weiwen). These migrant workers are largely employed in the manufacturing and construction industries. As the human force behind the urbanisation process they are its powerhouse, as well as its essential side effect. In the hundreds of factory towns scattered around China's developing regions, swelling migrant workers form an itinerant urban population and economy all of their own, in populations sometimes totalling a million people. China now has more than 166 cities with populations of at least a million, while the US has only nine such cities.[12]

In and around the city, existing farmland and villages have been replaced by areas that have become increasingly high density as farmers have used their land rights to become unlicensed property 'developers' building urbanised 'Villages in the City' (ViCs) to accommodate incoming migrants (see pp 52–5, Yushi Uehara, 'Unknown Urbanity; Towards the Village in the City'). The ViC phenomenon has presented a social and planning challenge to the authorities. Though the footprints of the 'villages' tend to be small in terms of the city as a whole, their social impact can be enormous. Where ViCs have been relocated to make way for new developments, providing housing for the migrant workers has become a particular problem as few have resident status and are not therefore eligible for social welfare benefits and public housing. The architectural practice URBANUS has conducted four studies of different ViCs in Shenzhen, which has 192 ViCs in total. These represent individual design proposals and a new housing type for low-income workers, which is economic in its construction while also providing social amenities that are reminiscent of the 1950s People's Communes (see pp 56–9, Meng Yan, 'Urban Villages'). So much tension exists in this urban context where there is often conflict between the drive to gentrify old districts and the need to accommodate migrant rural communities that inhabit the city without resident status or social welfare benefits. In 2005 central government attempted to address the widening income gap of 1:4 between rural and urban populations[13] by launching sympathetic policies proposing the building of 'New Socialist Villages' in rural areas to improve the existing social and physical infrastructure (see p 96, Sun Shiwen, Chronology).

Utopian Dreams and a Society of the Spectacle

In his article 'Leaving Utopian China' (pp 36–9), Zhou Rong points out that since the classical cities of ancient times Chinese society has been plagued by the desire to model itself on utopian ideals. This impulse extends itself to contemporary cities that are modelled on generic digital PowerPoint visualisations dressed up for marketing and political gain. In some places, these visions have manifested themselves in large-scale architectural models of an entire city, housed in impressive planning exhibition centres. The models themselves, however, cannot keep up with the reality outside on the construction site, which is changing faster than the show model can be adapted or modified.

The utopian urban model and city reality have a mutual effect, contributing to the creation of 'instant cities' that are either built on razed grounds or from scratch on agricultural land. Neville Mars conversely argues for the role of utopian dreams in the 'Chinese dream' (see pp 40–3, Neville Mars 'The Chinese City, A Self-Contained Utopia'), although he is also critical of these ambitions to fully urbanise in a single generation. He regards urbanisation itself as a utopian goal, and the new Chinese city as a utopian dream to rebuild society, as illustrated by central government's target to build 400 more cities by 2020 to achieve an urbanisation rate of 60 per cent from the current 44 per cent.[14]

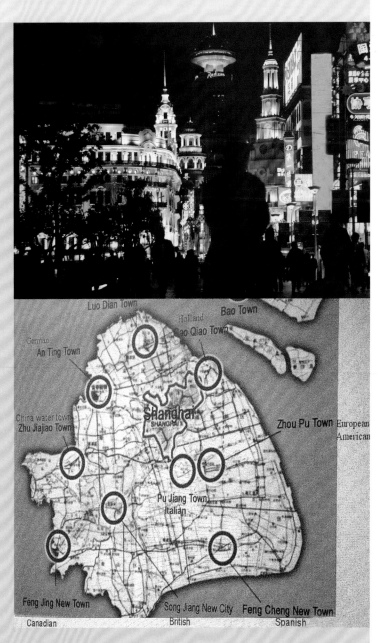

The domestic consumption boom in major cities (for example, in Shanghai's Nanjing Road, shown centre) has spawned new variations of 'Chinese contemporary living' and mutations of imported models of living environments and architectural styles. Shanghai's infamous 'one city nine towns' urban policy has resulted in the building of many culturally dislocated suburban 'themed towns'.

Mars also laments the unsustainability of building and destroying cities every generation with shifting political movements. The new middle-class workers now have new residential lifestyle aspirations – the most notorious being Shanghai's 'one city nine towns' development – whether it is living in mixed-use Central Business Districts (CBDs) or European-themed suburban villas connected by high-speed bullet trains. These emerging patterns of urban consumption indicate just how effective surreal fantasies and mass spectacle have become as marketing tools for selling generic architecture. However, they also represent a deeper-rooted 'coming out' of Chinese urban pride that demands ever more spectacular and different architectural designs. Event-city spectacles, such as the Olympic facilities in Beijing and entire themed towns, may have a lasting effect in raising the standards of design and construction locally, but they also often have a limited shelf life, and require more sustainable architectural design solutions. Should China's 'society of the spectacle' be viewing such fantastic and sometimes surreal urban interventions as culturally misaligned or heroic? Or should we be regarding them as the West's secret desire to export its urban fantasies abroad, when they are unable to fulfil them at home?

Resources, Expiry and Sustainable Futures

Global institutions such as the United Nations, World Health Organization and World Bank have published statistics on China's urban environmental damage and consumption patterns that point towards looming ecological disasters and energy shortages. Sixteen of the 20 most polluted cities in the world are now in China. By 2020 the country is expected to be the world's largest oil consumer; it is already one of the largest consumers of water and also the largest waste generator.[15] China faces insurmountable challenges that require a paradigm shift in the way it builds its cities and consumes energy as urbanised populations are sure to grow in scale and proportion of available land (see pp 72–3, Kyong Park). Signs of China's recent commitment have been demonstrated in the 2003 comprehensive sustainable development policies launched by the State Development and Reform Commission (following Beijing's pledge in 2001 to host a greener Olympics) and the setting up of the Ministry of Environmental Protection at the 2008 National People's Congress (NPC) as one of the five new 'Super Ministries'.

China has since begun to experiment with some of the most advanced ideas in sustainable design, such as Arup's near zero-carbon emission eco-city of Dongtan, near Shanghai (see pp 64–9, Helen Castle, 'Dongtan, China's Flagship Eco-city: An interview with Peter Head of

Urban spectacles in China are symbols of power and status, as well as being tourist attractions. Beijing has created an original spectacular architecture with its 'Bird's Nest' Olympic Stadium. And in Shenzhen we find surreal urban spectacles such as a scaled-down San Francisco Golden Gate Bridge among luxury residences next to replicas of world monuments.

Arup'). Another radical new city under planning and construction is Guangming New City (the Chinese name translates as 'radiant'), spearheaded by the Shenzhen Planning Bureau as a 'new radiant city' for China pushing experimental planning concepts, sustainable design and high-technology development.[16] The Danish–Chinese collaboration on sustainable urban development in China entitled 'Co-Evolution' won the Pavilion prize at the 2006 Venice Biennale where the project was exhibited.[17] However, the above efforts at sustainable environments do not yet deal with the problem of the inevitable expiry of a multitude of mono-type factory towns,[18] especially in the PRD where production costs are rising and low-end manufacturing is not economically sustainable.

The possibility of the mass exodus of millions of migrant workers who have contributed to the development and wealth of these cities is a cause for serious concern among planning authorities, requiring them to rethink the inflexible generic designs that currently proliferate in such towns. Four future urban models could be speculated here for urban China's future cities: the CCTV Headquarters designed by Rem Koolhaas, and 20 high-rise towers and three villas designed by Riken Yamamoto for the Jianwai SOHO residential business district, both in Beijing. These large-scale iconic structures accommodate self-contained, 24-hour globalised communities. Guangming New City shows how high-density living can be combined with environmental development. Songgan's new masterplan proposal by CUHK Urbanisation Studio (a project led by Laurence Liauw)[19] attempts to resist the expiry of a typical PRD factory town through typological transformations. URBANUS' radical adaptation of a vernacular housing type from Fujian Province similarly accommodates changes in use, providing low-cost social housing for migrant workers.

The 2008 earthquake tragedy in Sichuan Province, and devastating spring snowstorms over the new year, have also created widespread destruction and the need to rebuild hundreds of thousands of buildings and public infrastructure. This coming challenge offers a chance for authorities to rethink their planning strategies for affected communities in order to provide safer construction with better environmental control and improved infrastructure in case of natural disasters.

As new development in Chinese cities requires almost endless quantities of building materials and natural resources, China has begun to experiment with sustainable design approaches and materials recycling (top image). In response to central government's introduction of sustainable development policies, Shenzhen city organised the 'Global 500 Environmental Forum' in 2002 (bottom image).

After China: Exporting China

Despite China's urban prosperity today, some critics have been asking 'What happens After China?'... India, Russia, Vietnam, Mexico?[20] Three tenets of Chinese cities – industrialisation, modernisation and urbanisation – can either happen in sequence as in the West, or sometimes overlap in time. Globalisation of world cities has meant that capital moves freely and rapidly around the world seeking returns on investment that could be insensitive to local politics and culture. It is worth asking now some critical questions of China's seemingly unstoppable urban expansion and gradual exporting of the effects of this urbanisation to other countries (see pp 70–81, Kyong Park, Laurence Liauw and Doreen Heng Liu, 'After China, the World?'). Will the major players in China's booming cities start to operate beyond its borders? Will the Chinese process and pattern of urbanisation, especially SEZs, be repeated in other developing countries? Will global capital merely bring with it generic forms of urbanism that are tailored to China and re-exported as urban products, but not culture? Will the Chinese urbanisation machine eventually run out of steam and be forced to export its excess production capacity overseas like factories do? Is the Planned Economy and SEZs built from zero a unique Chinese model that could be applied elsewhere in a different culture? Does utopian urban ambition care about the future sustainability of society, and if not then how will one generation's Utopia become another's burden? If the world is showing some signs of Sinofication while China is being globalised, then how will China generate its own urban culture to become an empire of ideas again? Could the new Chinese urban taxonomies proposed by Jiang Jun[21] (see also pp 16–21) spawn hybrids and interactions in other urban cultures in years to come? Could the informal urbanism that characterises China today eventually become a cultural diaspora like that of Chinese migrants working both within and outside their own country? Doreen Heng Liu (see pp 18–81) takes us back to the 'generic cities' of the PRD[22] where it all started 30 years ago, claiming that Deng Xiaoping could be China's 'New Urbanist'. She suggests that it is the fearless 'ideology' of the PRD with its scenarios of expiry and rebirth that is the truly exportable urban concept, but only if this product of the new city becomes cultivated. (This theme was recently investigated in the Ma Qingyun-curated 2007 Shenzhen Biennale of Architecture and Urbanism, 'COER' – as city of expiry and regeneration.)[23] Thus the main essays of this issue of *AD* end where new urban China started – in Southern China's Pearl River Delta – where an open lab of urban experimentation over the past 30 years has brought about China's '*real leap forward*' and allowed '*a hundred cities to bloom*'. **ᗡ**

It is conceivable that future Chinese cities could develop in four possible directions.
Top left: Rem Koolhaas' CCTV Headquarters and Riken Yamamoto's proposal for the Jianwai SOHO residential business district, both in Beijing, represent contemporary approaches to transforming iconic structures into self-contained, 24-hour globalised communities.
Top right: The Guangming New City proposal by architects MVRDV shows how high-density living can be combined with sustainable environmental development.
Bottom left: Songgan town's new 2015 masterplan proposal by CUHK resists the future extinction of mono-type factory towns via design flexibility and typological transformation of the urban plan.
Bottom right: URBANUS' adaptation of a vernacular housing type from Fujian Province mutates into low-cost housing that provides basic accommodation for migrant workers and mixed-use public amenities within the compound.

Farmland in the Pearl River Delta sits among an urbanised landscape of factories and urban villages that eventually become towns of up to a million people. Numerous PRD factory towns (such as Songgan, shown here) specialise in a single or just a few manufactured products, causing serious environmental pollution. As rising wages cause a decline in the competitiveness of PRD industries, the survival of these Southern China boom towns is now under threat.

Notes

1. Political slogans from leaders in China determine official policies even before they are drafted as law. *Great Leap Forward* was one of Chairman Mao's policies in the 1950s to overtake Western countries in terms of national production output. '*To get rich is glorious*' was Deng Xiaoping's mantra in 1978 launching economic reforms, and '*Let a hundred flowers bloom*' (*flowers* modified to *cities* in this article) was Chairman Mao's philosophy that promoted progress and diverse schools of thought in the 1950s.

2. Danish Architecture Centre (curators), *Co-Evolution*, Danish Architecture Centre publication for 10th Venice Architecture Biennale, 2006; Worldwatch Institute Report, 2006 (www.worldwatch.org/pubs/sow/2006); UNDP, WHO, World Bank statistics 2004, 2005, 2006.

3. Anthony Yeh et al (eds), *Developing a Competitive Pearl River Delta*, Hong Kong University Press, 2006.

4. Laurence Liauw, 'Shenzhen City Focus', *World Architecture*, October 1998.

5. Rem Koolhaas, 'Introduction' in Chuihua Judy Chung, Jeffrey Inaba, Rem Koolhaas and Sze Tsung Leong (eds), *Great Leap Forward: Harvard Design School Project on the City*, Taschen GmbH, 2001.

6. Danish Architecture Centre op cit.

7. Caijing Annual Edition, *China 2008 Forecasts and Strategies*, Caijing Magazine, pp 18–20, 115–16, 120–21, 124–25, 164–67. See also Lauren Parker and Zhang Hongxing (eds), *China Design Now*, V&A Publishing, 2008.

8. D Farrell, J Devan and J Woetzel, 'Where Big is Best', *Newsweek Magazine*, 26 May–2 June 2008, pp 45–6 (reference to McKinsey Global Institute).

9. See http://www.opendemocracy.net/arts-photography/hutong_destruction_3632.jsp and www.iht.com/articles/2007/08/03/news/beijing.php.

10. Farrell, Devan and Woetzel op cit.

11. Ole Bouman (ed), in *Volume 8: Ubiquitous China*, Archis, No 2, 2006.

12. Ibid.

13. *National Geographic Atlas of China*, 2008.

14. Neville Mars, in *Cities from Zero*, AA Publications, 2006, pp 105–12.

15. Danish Architecture Centre op cit.

16. Guangming New City International Competition documents, Shenzhen Planning Bureau, 2007.

17. Danish Architecture Centre op cit.

18. *National Geographic – Chinese Edition*, May 2008, pp 176–80 (reference by Peter Hessler on the genesis of China's factory towns).

19. Laurence Liauw with CUHK Urbanization Studio, Post-Industrial Urbanism: PRD Factory Town, exhibited at the Shenzhen Biennale of Architecture & Urbanism, 2007.

20. 'Exporting China' Symposium at Columbia University Graduate School of Architecture and Planning, with Mark Wigley, Yung Ho Chang, Ma Qingyun, Ackbar Abbass and Doreen Liu, 16 Feb 2008. The contents of this article do not make any direct reference to the forum contents, although some of the themes investigated may overlap.

21. Jiang Jun (ed), 'We Make Cities', *Urban China* magazine, Issue 04, 2005.

22. Rem Koolhaas, 'Pearl River Delta/10 Years Later', *Urban China* magazine, Issue 13, 2006, pp 14, 118.

23. 2nd Shenzhen Biennale of Architecture & Urbanism, 2007. See http://www.szhkbiennale.org/2007/eng.

The Taxonomy of Contemporary Chinese Cities (We Make Cities)
A Sampling

Rem Koolhaas famously highlighted the uniformity of Chinese cities with his identification of 'the generic city' in the Pearl River Delta in the 1990s. Here Jiang Jun, Editor-in-Chief of *Urban China* magazine, and Kuang Xiaoming highlight the 'unified diversity' and complexity of contemporary urbanism through his own system of classification.

The official logo of *Urban China* magazine represents its ambition, through its publications and activities, to interpret 'Chinese characteristics' and 'Chinese-ness' as its copyright.

Unified Diversity and the Urban Knowledge Tree

In order to classify Chinese cities, it is necessary to recognise that this 'Chinese-ness' has to be balanced out between two extremes: firstly the size of China's territory and the length of its history, which have generated considerable diversity; secondly, the power that governs this diversity, which has always been highly centralised. (Hierarchical rule represents a significant tradition for Chinese civilisation, but also an ideological inertia.) Behind this 'unified diversity' is the Chinese philosophy 'seeking common ground, while allowing for minor differences'. This is as deeply embedded in the minds of Chinese people as the space of Chinese cities themselves. It enables an urban taxonomy in which the Darwinian model of hierarchy of the species can be introduced to map out the origin of Chinese cities.

The differentiations in the functioning of cities are an upshot of the distribution of the macro-planned administrative structure. It is also a matter of self-evolution in the competition for the 'survival of the fittest'. The knowledge tree behaves like a 'general map' of the taxonomy of contemporary Chinese cities and reveals the interrelationships between them in the form of the network they weave within their common Chinese context. It is not a geographical map but a knowledge tree that analyses and defines the complexity of Chinese cities, so that the visible and the invisible, reality and super-reality, modern and pre-modern, structure and superstructure are able to share a common platform. Every node in the map (like hypertext links) becomes a collection point for common strands. The taxonomy of contemporary Chinese cities weaves a panorama of diverse contexts through an unravelling of this hypertext, just like the Darwinian taxonomy of biological systems. This urban taxonomy could pave the way for an 'urbanology of new urban China'.

Migration City
This is a city with a mobile population, or a 'city on the move with the people inhabiting it'. There is either an attraction here or a driving force elsewhere to keep the city/people moving; thus it is about the dynamic inequality between both ends of the migration, as well as the insertion of an alternative content (people) into another context (city).

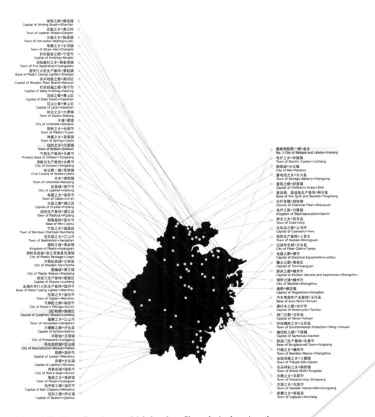

Map of Zhejiang Province, which borders Shanghai, showing the numerous entrepreneurial, self-organised one-product towns – those which focus on the manufacture of one product only and occupy a large share of the market for that particular product.

Macro-Planning

Centralism in government always leads to the prioritisation of planning in the urbanisation process. When planning is top-down beyond the city itself, it becomes 'macro-planning'. China's planning has been projected at a national strategic level both in feudal times and under communist rule. The configuration of urban policy has been determined either through social institutions from Confucian ideology (which for elders and social superiors was a major tenet) or as administrative commands through government sanctioned by 'red-titled file' directives from the Planned Economy. The city in feudal times was developed through a 'courtyard house' model designated by the emperor, and in socialist times it was developed through a 'workshop model' designated by national industries. As the Chinese city was not a city with its own civil independence, it is necessary to define the macro-planned Chinese city within its social and physical context.

Hi-China

Urban China's Hi-China (a general taxonomy) is a database of surveys of 100 Chinese cities that includes more than 500,000 photographs. It is also a general directory that is intended to operate as a whole, reflecting the multiplicity of Chinese cities and offering the most efficient way of managing, and searching for them. Not only can this generic directory instantly classify the large numbers of images from each city, it also generates links between the different cities by recognising the parallel relationships between them, such as the urban activities of dwelling, producing and consuming. As the subdirectories of all levels are simultaneously a series of independent urban projects, Hi-China is gradually evolving into a 'project of projects', in which each project can be linked to all those cities that share the same segments of knowledge. In this way the invisibility of order is indicated by the visibility of the phenomenon: the super-reality is constructed by the ordinary and trivial reality.

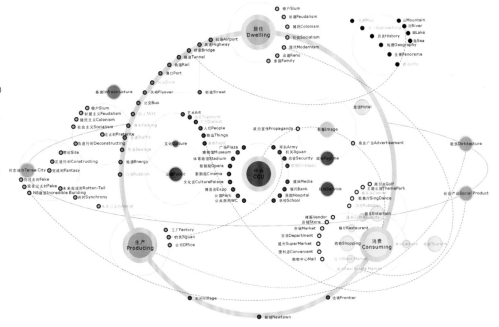

Special Economic Zone (SEZ)
The SEZs were the first Chinese coastal cities to be shaped by market reform in the early 1980s through market-driven, instead of politically motivated, development. Their geographical locations demonstrate the clear ambition to attract foreign investment. However, the benefits they received in terms of preferential policy have been weakened in recent years with the further opening up of the hinterland cities. Shown here is a famous street poster depicting Deng Xiaoping's reforms for Shenzhen.

Boom–Bust

The Open Door signals that Deng Xiaoping communicated through his second tour of Southern China in 1992, when he visited Guangzhou, Shenzhen, Zhuhai and Shanghai making speeches that reasserted his reformist economic policies, were soon taken up by the whole country. One after another, almost every city started to build its own small 'Special Economic Zone' (SEZ). These 'development zones' generated important tax revenues. Ironically, in the mid-1990s China's largest economic zone, Hainan, lost its leading position in an economic bubble created by the real-estate market, and became a failed experiment – a 'rotten-tail city' with thousands of square metres of unfinished building sites. However, the 'Hainan Lesson' did not spread across the whole country like the successful 'Shenzhen Experience' did. Obviously, with development zones flourishing throughout the country, some cities became 'little Shenzhens', while some others inevitably became 'little Hainans'. This only goes to show the double-edged effect of an 'informal economy' based on market principles with loose governance.

Rotten-Tail City
This is when a city-making movement is frozen by the collapse of the economic ecosystem during a bubble economy. Enough half-constructed buildings and infrastructure litters the urban landscape to make it the city incomplete.

'Chinese characteristics' mark the localisation of Marxism and Leninism, which were introduced from the Western world at the beginning of the last century and were interpreted first into the context of Maoism, and later the reformist theories of Deng Xiaoping. Shenzhen is waving farewell to its adolescence after 30 years of successful rapid development, gradually transforming from a hot-blooded and impulsive SEZ into a more rational and mature city. Shown here is the cover of the *Urban China* Special Issue on Regenerating Shenzhen (Issue 24, 2007).

Collective Space

To unify urban diversities is to introduce the generic into the specific. Macro-planning deploys the state's generic urban programmes and planning structure across the borders of individual regions. Once the prototype of the city is set up as a developing model, it can be generalised through a centrally managed system. As the genesis of most cities was created under the same patriarchal system, similar forms of urban living and functioning operations – both mass-produced – could be easily found even among distant and dissimilar cities. So in these different cities, parallel lives of sameness can be regarded as taking place in a self-organising way. The spatial structure of these generic cities mutates with time, while the parallelity of similar lives and urban activities in between them can be seen as a collective heritage from the socialist policies of the past. In this regard, the taxonomy of Chinese cities becomes legible as a universal subdirectory that is based on a generic spatial structure.

Once a self-sufficient and isolated island China despite its recent ambitious globalisation process, remains deeply affected by colonialism, communism, global industrial transfer and the financial markets. Globalisation is diluting China's 'uniqueness' (its national character), and this is being replaced with homogeneous parallel universes of urban phenomena co-existing simultaneously both in China and in certain countries abroad (communism, the Great Leap Forward, science cities, instant cities, the People's Commune, shrinking cities, mega-dams, Olympic cities and so on), reflecting the parallelity of China's collective fate with that of the rest of the world. Shown here is the cover of the *Urban China* Special Issue on the Parallel Universe (Issue 26, 2008).

Deconstructed City
The reverse action (demolition) of city-making is actually a preparation for constructing the city. 'The constructed' that replaces 'the demolished' with new content needs to match the original value of the targeted demolished urban sites but with new added values. This is a so-called 'victory' of the purely economic value of new zoning plans compared to the historic value of the existing architecture and urban fabric.

Generic Model

As contemporary Chinese cities can be regarded as sharing a common structure of space and time, a generic model can be set up to categorise any of these types of cities. The Modernist classification of urban activities – living, working, shopping and transporting – is still feasible in configuring a triangular circulation model, while the 'Chinese characteristic' of the administration-oriented city-making model is emphasised by the CCU (central controlling unit) in the political core. Public spaces and social services, provided either by the government or by society, are distributed in between. The dimension of politicised urban timelines – feudalism, colonialism, socialism and post-socialism – influences stacked layers of the whole city structure, thereby acting as a counterforce of 'tabula rasa Modernism'. A generic urban model is an all-inclusive envelope for a number of cities to be interconnected node-to-node, integrating them into a hyper-system of cities.

Factory-Product City

This is a mono-type city that revolves around the manufacture of a certain group of products. The urban lifeline is also the product line, and the inhabitants are the workers, who with their families work on the same type of products. In the recent wave of urbanisation this has become the most common type of city generation. A mono-type city is producing, while the city itself is also being produced by a specific product. It either has an integrated production line, or is within a region with a larger production framework. A factory-product city is always identified with its product, expanding and shrinking physically with export-market fluctuations elsewhere in the world.

Overwritten Time

Over the last century, the revolution/reformation of Chinese modernisation has left at least four gradual stages that articulate the *Zeitgeist* in the 'dynastic history' of Chinese cities: feudalism, colonialism, socialism and post-socialism. Time, as another dimension, provides multiple layers of spatial structure. It is a game of overwritten times and a battle of mutated *Zeitgeists*. Taxonomy of urban space is also archaeology of time. Each category of space is stacked within the coexistence of old and new, the collision between the 'Brave New World' and Modernism, and the regeneration of the old within the new.

Micro-Society and Self-Centered Urbanism

Diversity comes from asymmetric developments in the various stages of evolution. A single node of a city can be complex enough to be an independent micro-society, for example a slum area as an enclave or as an industrial 'factory-product city' – a local part becomes the actual whole. The logic of fractal science could be applied here to generate an urban subdirectory mirroring the structure of the root directory of the whole city, which is sometimes not much more than the subdirectory itself. Because of the correspondence between the local part and the actual whole, a node-to-node mirror image of a certain city part can be set up for taxonomic comparison.

Micro-society provides the potential for local metropolitan areas to gain the integrity of a city and become the city itself. As the multidimensionality of China provides a spectrum of city typologies, there are always extreme cases in which a new urbanism can evolve from anywhere and almost anything: a sleeping dormitory city, army city, factory city, port city, shopping city, immigrant city', 'university city', theme park city, 'event city', 'village city', 'geometric city' or even a construction-site city. It is not the extremeness of each single case, but the overall balance of the urban ecological system in which every starting point has the potential to be the centre that constitutes a taxonomy of Chinese cities.

University City

This city is formed out of a single university, or several universities clustered together on one site. It has the usual functions to match the integrated composition of an entire city. The consumption of its population, as well as the magnetic pull of its national and international cultural economy, make it an important governmental gambling chip for the catalytic development of a new, much larger-scale city around the university.

Event City

This is a city generated or strengthened by a specific mega-event, which provides a platform for the extraordinary injection of funds around the designated time and place of the event, and where disproportionate resources are invested in order to maximise the energy of the event. Sometimes the physical resources and infrastructure produced are massive enough to generate a new city in itself, or to regenerate an old city. A related variation is the theme park city, which provides Arcadias of exoticism, where dwellers are only consumers and tourists instead of permanent residents.

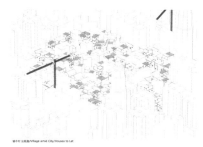

Village City

The village city is the physical product of the conflict between rapid urbanisation and the urban-rural duality of the planned economy. Massive amounts of built-up infill are placed on rural land, which results in the collective construction efforts of the villagers, who build private houses on the site of their urban village motivated by potential rental income. This type of informal implosion provides affordable spaces for the poor immigrant labour force and creates a dense, chaotic or even terrifying urbanscape in the government-organised scene of a new city under construction.

Geometric Cities: Plaza City/Axis City

The plaza city (often empty) has the ability to process public activities such as gathering, inspecting, commemorating and exhibiting, so that the space expresses patriarchy and custodianship through the symbolism of its very conspicuous absence. The axis city (shown here) emphasises the centre of power and its extension. Its conscious expression of the government's achievement becomes a critical tool in the reinforcement of the city's identity and form. ☼

The Institutional and Political Background to Chinese Urbanisation

Chinese cities have a very distinct history defined by their relationship to government and the land. Under imperial rule they served as administrative centres for rural agricultural areas that took precedence, economically and politically. Professor **Sun Shiwen** of Tongji University, Shanghai, describes how today's urbanisation process is still informed by the city's uniquely Chinese characteristics.

Old city streets of Shanghai compete and coexist with new developments.

An inner-city construction site within the demolished old city fabric, Shanghai.

Most of those who migrate to the city from the countryside do not become city dwellers. Consequently, they move from one city to another, and after several years they return to their native land in the countryside.

The notion of what constitutes a city in China is very different to that of the West. This relates back to imperial rule before the 20th century when the foundation of Chinese cities was based on the needs of the administrative system of government. Cities were founded only where primary government was, and the size of a city was entirely dependent on the classification of the government. When a city was formed, administration offices and city walls were built first; the government offices being at the centre of the city. Rich families of merchants and administrative officials of the imperial court would be moved in nearby, and service industries as required, so people with skills became part of the city. The Chinese city was firstly an administrative centre on which consumption depended, with incomes being drawn from farming the land. It belonged to the wealthy citizens such as administrative officers, merchant traders, and noblemen and their extended families, who strictly controlled it behind its walls, keeping most of the people from outside away.

Economically speaking there were more people who lived off agriculture in the countryside, thus rural areas played an important role in the provision of food and income tax. They contributed to the steadiness and security of the nation. As a result, the government at all levels paid more attention to rural areas. Methods of management that emerged in the development of agriculture were often applied directly to the city during imperial periods prior to the 20th century, an effect that continues to the present day. When Chinese people refer to '*chengshi*' ('city' in the Chinese language), the administrative area includes not only city areas (in the Western sense), but also extensive rural areas under the same administration. Thus methods of urban management, even since the 1950s, such as the organisation of massive shifts in China's government policies, are similar to large group exercises in the rural agricultural fields.

China's very distinct, historical urban model has meant that it has also urbanised in a very different way to the West. For example, while large numbers of people have moved to the city from rural areas (cities such as Shanghai or Shenzhen now have populations of more than 18 million and 12 million and rising, up from around 12 million and 5 million a decade ago), they are still not registered as citizens in governmental or urban statistics; instead, they are treated as a special group of 'migrant workers'. Most of those who migrate to the city from the countryside do not become city dwellers. Consequently, they move from one city to another, and after several years they return to their native land in the countryside. Despite this, the number of registered city dwellers is growing dramatically; what official statistics cannot reveal is the number of people on the move, which would have a large impact on the official urbanisation rate.

Migrant labourers and the newly built city, Shanghai.

Public participation in urban planning, Jiaxing, Zhejiang Province.

NPC (National People's Congress) and CPPC (Chinese People's Political Consultative Conference) live televised event, 2008.
Major central government policies are decided and announced at this event to the entire country, and set in motion actions from various Chinese authorities at all levels.

Hukou Census Registers

China's current policy of issuing census registers, or *hukou* (household accounts), evolved from a population management system established in the 1950s to meet the demands for control of the Communist Party's Planned Economy, a system whereby the entire population was divided into two non-interchangeable groups: rural *hukou* and non-rural *hukou* (registered 'citizens'). Under the Planned Economy, the rural lived in the countryside and made a living by themselves, while the non-rural lived in cities, with daily necessities supplied by the nation in the form of commodity rations.

The marketisation and Open Door policies introduced by China's leader, Deng Xiaoping, from 1978 and throughout the 1980s did not change the established policy of the census register. Though there were no longer restrictions on peasants coming to the city for work, their activities in urban areas were still circumscribed by their classification as the 'rural population'. They were not afforded the same welfare benefits and public services as citizens, and were still treated as 'migrant' or 'peasant' workers. Currently, the number of this 'floating population' nationwide is estimated between 140 million and 200 million; it is largely concentrated in eastern coastal cities as well as other major metropolitan areas. Cities such as Beijing and Shanghai have more than 3 million migrant workers, while in Shenzhen the number is close to 5 million.

The official urbanisation rate is the ratio of registered urban citizens to the whole population, which discounts those who live and work in the city without being included in the census register. Since the late 1990s, a new classification of 'permanent resident' has been introduced for those who have worked and lived in the city for more than six months. According to the census of 2000, the national urbanisation rate was 36.22 per cent, though this would be considerably higher if it were to include rural newcomers to the city.

Government Administrative Management

In the past, the system of Chinese government administrative management has tended towards centralisation. The Open Door policies of the 1980s, however, introduced a process of decentralisation, giving local government a wider range of powers. Although the central government still plays a major role in macro-control policy and the coordination of large industries and utilities, most local governments can now choose their own urban development types and real-estate development in cities. The general plans of large cities must still be approved by the State Council of the People's Republic of China, though local authorities can govern planning implementation. Central government controls the developmental activities in rural areas rigidly, especially in terms of protecting cultivated land.

Chinese urban policy is determined by the nation's executive, which is made up of provinces, municipalities and autonomous regions. Municipalities are part of the organisational system of a city, but have the same power as a province. Provinces and autonomous regions are composed of cities and autonomous prefectures, consisting of counties and county-level cities. There are districts in the municipality and the prefecture-level cities as well. Representing each of these for urban development are planning bureaus at local city level (city government), with provincial secretaries (provincial government) and state ministries (central government) at the national level of representation.

In 1994, a reformation of the taxation system affected the raising and distribution of land value-added taxes. This has enhanced central government's control over local income tax arising from land revenues, while local governments have expanded into the development of areas such as tertiary industry and real estate. These tax reforms encouraged local governments to become more actively involved in commercial forms of property development either through land auctions, tender or direct negotiation, as it was now necessary for them to be more market-driven.

While local government administration varies from region to region, the management of city planning follows two basic models: one is centralised management, such as in Beijing, Shenzhen and Guangzhou, where the planning department of the city government is in charge and the prefecture-level government has no say; and the other, represented by Shanghai and Qingdao, is shared management between the city and the prefecture (the planning department of the city government is in charge of planning and controlling key zoned projects, and the prefecture government controls development).

Land Policy

The development of land in urban areas depends on centrally controlled land-use policy. The marketisation of urban land began at the end of the 1980s, when state-owned land could be put up for leasehold sale. Through the repossession of state-owned land-use rights, the city government was able to raise considerable funds that were, in turn, assigned to large-scale construction projects. The fact that there is no system of fixed-asset taxation in Chinese cities means that governments cannot raise regular property income, so reselling state lands has become an ever more important means of raising funds for construction projects.

Through the remising of state land-use rights, private enterprises and overseas companies can invest in the construction of the city, enabling city planning to meet the demands from various sectors and enhance development of the city. With economic globalisation, Chinese cities have become the target of global capital: 'hot money' has swarmed into cities, placing considerable pressure on the Chinese economy.

Improvements in the real-estate market have encouraged central government to shift housing production away from public ownership to the private sector (private housing is called 'consumer housing'). Housing conditions have generally improved: the average living space in Shanghai has increased from less than 4 square metres (43 square feet) in 1980 to 16 square metres (172.2 square feet). However, with inflationary property prices in big cities, it has become more difficult for middle- and low-income citizens to afford decent housing. Central government has responded to this social problem by implementing housing macro-controls to curb price increases.

According to Chinese law, land is collectively owned and cannot be resold directly. It is only after appropriation by the government that land can be remised as land-use rights transfer between users – an upshot of the ruralurban binary system of the past; urban construction can only be successful by controlling rural land. Through the process of urbanisation, rural land has been consumed by high-speed development, and consequently stricter policies of rural land protection have now been adopted through national land policy.

Since the reform and Open Door policies of 1978 onwards, and as a result of globalisation and marketisation, China's cities have changed dramatically, and are experiencing rapidly rising urbanisation rates. However, traditional methods of administration – policies and strategies that focus mainly on the speed of economic growth – are still impacting city development, leading to both social and environmental problems. The recent application of macro-control policies on commercial land-use development to provide affordable housing and to protect the environment is only one of the few examples of central government attempting to adjust the trend of excessive urban development now sweeping the country. ⌂

Shanghai's North Bund historic riverfront district under construction.

Urbanisation in Contemporary

Shenzhen is one of the fastest-growing cities in China, having leapt from fishing village to a global city in a matter of a couple of decades. Here **Huang Weiwen**, the Deputy Director of the Urban and Architecture Department at Shenzhen Municipal Planning Bureau, provides the background to China's unrivalled urbanisation, which is unmatched in terms of both its speed and intensity.

Shenzhen's rapid development over the past 20 years began in the Lowu central area near the border crossing with Hong Kong.

China Observed Dramatic Changes and Disruptions

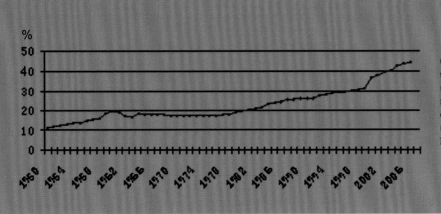

Chart showing the rate of urbanisation in China (1950–2007): percentage of registered inhabitants of cities compared to total population. (Data from China's National Bureau of Statistics.)

Intellectual young people in China were sent to work in the rural villages during the reformation of the 1960s.

In the less than 30 years since 1980, the number of urban citizens in China has increased by 400 million, and urbanisation has risen from 19.4 per cent to 43.9 per cent in 2006. This makes the intense rate and immense speed of urbanisation in China the country's most impressive feature.

The great watershed for the politicisation of Chinese society and economic institutions occurred in 1949 when the nascent communist regime was established with '*the rural besieging of the urban*'; cities came to be regarded as the beachhead of capitalism and were strictly controlled. In the 30 years that followed, development of cities stagnated and even partly regressed (they increased by only 8 per cent in total, and in the 12 years after 1960 actually fell by 2.6 per cent). In 1980, the rate of Chinese urbanisation, at 20 per cent, was less than half that of most developed countries, and was less than two-thirds that of other developing countries.

The reasons for this urban stagnation can be outlined as follows: (1) the replication of the Soviet model of the Planned Economy, which concentrated on excessive targeted outputs from agriculture and relatively developed cities (such as Shanghai). This had accumulated initial capital injections for China's rapid industrialisation, but had not been conducive to the healthy and sustainable development of agriculture and cities. China drew income mainly from agriculture and the acceleration of industrialisation. This was done through the accumulation of basic industries in developed cities, producing capital requirements for domestic output and generating national tax levies. In doing so the developed cities gradually helped transform China from an agriculture-based country to an industrialised one; (2) the Cold War and China's national strategy which set aside the development of coastal cities to focus resources on the construction of inland military cities (the so-called 'Third Front' cities); (3) the introduction of population management in 1958 with the *hukou* (a system of household registration and urban administration that strictly tied a person's resident status to a particular town or village, and restricted free rural migration to the cities; (4) the 1960s policy of sending urban young people to work on the land in the countryside or mountains, which endured for 25 years and became a 'counter-urbanisation' process that evacuated 20 million urban citizens and relieved the problem of unemployment in the cities.

In 1978, a new process of Chinese urbanisation was started by Deng Xiaoping's Open Door Policy, a process that was to accelerate in 1992. During the initial phase of the policy in the 1980s, the economic reformation was carried out in rural areas, and the nation

Street graffiti by migrant workers owed factory wages who wanted to go 'home' for the Chinese New Year.

explored economic growth through the model of the Planned Economy by establishing Special Economic Zones (SEZs) in coastal cities (opening up the market to trade, communication and investment with the outside world) and forming village enterprises in the villages and towns. The new industries in the SEZs absorbed a lot of redundant labour caused by the economic reforms in the rural regions. Alongside the widely accepted new policy of '*upgrading the official administrative status of places from big county to city, and big village to township*', the total population of towns and cities increased. '*Leaving the countryside for the city, and the village for the town*' caused the official administrative status of villages to shift and become more urbanised as they were assimilated into expanding cities' urban territories, or as the result of returning migrant workers building town-like settlements. They became 'big villages' and then later upgraded to 'township' status, again increasing the total population of towns and cities. Flourishing village enterprises increased the number of urban people, as many enterprise managers had the opportunity to change their peasant status to citizen status. However, the core concept of urban development was to '*control the scale of large cities, modest development of medium-size cities and active*

Alongside the widely accepted new policy of '*upgrading the official administrative status of places from big county to city, and big village to township*', the total population of towns and cities increased. '*Leaving the countryside for the city, and the village for the town*' caused the official administrative status of villages to shift and become more urbanised as they were assimilated into expanding cities' urban territories, or as the result of returning migrant workers building town-like settlements.

development of small cities'. This encouraged peasants to 'leave the land without emigrating from the village; and work in factories without settling in cities', since they could keep their rural land even as they worked in the cities.

As mentioned above, economic growth and urbanisation in China began to accelerate in 1992. Dissatisfied with the slowing economic reform after the tragic Tiananmen Square protests of 1989, Deng Xiaoping appealed for 'bigger reform steps to be taken' and specified 'development as an essential criterion'. The socialist market economy now began to allow the buying and selling of land through the transfer of land-use rights and this combined with the speedy expansion of new urban areas and the productive use of the land with cheap human resources, transformed China into an economic wonderland and a 'production factory of the world' for overseas investment.

More than 200 million people have moved to major cities over the past 14 years. However, between 150 million and 300 million unregistered migrant workers (called the 'floating population') remain unaccounted for in the urbanisation process. This is the most outstanding characteristic of disruption in China's urbanisation process. The industrialisation process, with low wages and poor welfare, is insufficient to maintain living standards for those on low incomes in the cities. With the restriction of permanent migration to the cities, migratory peasant workers become the primary labour force supporting urbanisation, instead of its targeted population. With no sense of belonging in the cities within which they work, migrant peasant workers only have time once a year to return to their village homelands for a family reunion during the Chinese New Year holidays. This annual spring festival migration means up to 200 million passengers travel over a period of just 40 days. In February 2008, an unprecedented disastrous snowstorm in Southern China interrupted this mass migration and caused serious casualities, both human and in terms of the country's infrastructure, that affected the whole of China.

Cities review their hukou household registration system and population policies in order to restrict the freedom of migrant workers settling in cities. However, a diverse mix of social classes is necessary

Chaos at train stations as migrant workers try to return home in the 2008 snowstorm.

Shenzhen's Futian central administration district developed in the 1990s during the city's economic boom and has continued to do so over the following 10 years, to the present day.

Government policy has been driven by the industrialisation of the national economy, with urbanisation only a by-product with disruptive side effects. Urbanisation could instead be a policy in itself, with industrialisation as a by-product.

for a city to function properly. Thus we should reflect critically on the current urban policy of excluding working-class migrant workers via the *hukou* system, so that urban societies can become more balanced and be sustained. When urban land and material resources are concentrated on industrialisation for GDP growth, cheap labour is necessary, and urbanisation becomes a by-product of this. Cities become industrial agglomerations for migrant workers without urban status, while urbanisation is treated merely as a strategy for economic building through industrialisation. Government policy has been driven by the industrialisation of the national economy, with urbanisation only a by-product with disruptive side effects. Urbanisation could instead be a policy in itself, with industrialisation as a by-product.

With the overexpansion of the cities and rapid industrialisation comes another feature of urbanisation: disruption to the environment. According to current World Bank statistics, Chinese cities are frequently in the top 10 most polluted cities in the world. The Taihu Lake pollution crisis in the Yangtse River Delta, which affected the drinking-water supply of about 2 million residents in Eastern China, and the red tides (caused by high concentrations of algae and affecting agricultural production) in the Pearl River Delta have in recent years demonstrated how severe such ecological damage is now becoming.

Another important characteristic of Chinese urbanisation is the disruption caused by subjective

strategy compared with objective reality. The 1950s policy of blindly chasing industrial output figures turned cities of consumption into cities of production, and caused cities such as Beijing, the administrative and cultural centre, to become an industrial city with low productivity. After the not so constructive Third Front cities policies of the 1960s and 1970s, in the 1980s and 1990s attention shifted to the development of large cities, an urban policy that also placed emphasis on the development of smaller towns. But the poor efficiency of such smaller towns resulted in failure. Since 2000, due to continued higher growth in major cities, government policy has focused on building repetitive mega-cities and regional urban agglomerations. However, interurban networks remain inadequate, thus the mega-cities, medium cities and small cities cannot develop coherently.

The above disruptions are essentially all the result of the Planned Economy, which put too much emphasis on central control and the macro-planning of the economy over city planning. At the same time, they reveal how inexperienced Chinese city planning is, both in theory and in practice. Central government is now attempting to correct the excesses of certain economy-oriented ideas by advocating a policy of scientific development in the context of a people-oriented and harmonious society, where new planning strategies for the urban and the rural consider both as a coordinated whole. If China can rise to these challenges and urbanisation can grow in a balanced and steady way without disruption, the national urbanisation rate should eventually reach the target level of other developed countries (China is targeting around 60 per cent by 2020), and some one billion urban residents can settle in cities and live a better life. ⚫

Urbanisation in China

in the Age of Reform

Urban China today has been shaped by industrialisation and economic reform. Professor **Zhang Jie** from the School of Architecture at Tshinghua University, Beijing, describes how a market-driven process has resulted not only in uneven regional development across the country, but also in a lack of coherency in planning at the local level.

Industrialisation, which has made China the world's factory that it is today, has to be seen as the fundamental force behind the urbanisation process that has been under way since the late 1970s. The township industries that were triggered by rural reforms and the introduction of Special Economic Zones (SEZs) in the coastal regions in the early 1980s shook the existing state-run industrial base. Fast-growing industrial townships played a major part in convincing the government that the small-town approach to urbanisation was a successful one. These SEZs, especially in the Pearl River Delta (PRD) and Yangtze River Delta, later became key industrial bases for world manufacturing. Booming industrial parks flourished in 14 pilot coastal open cities, later spreading to the surrounding second-tier cities, and recently inland to Western China.

Economic reforms with preferential policies shaped China's unbalanced regional developments from the east to the west, creating complicated urban–rural relationships at the regional level.[1,2] The massive flow of rural migrants from the inland areas to the coastal regions has become a dominant force of China's current urbanisation.[3] The millions of rural migrants in the PRD, and the very existence of urban villages, are just the most well-known examples (see Yushi Uehara and Meng Yan's articles on the Village in the City (ViC), on pp 52–5 and 56–9).

This unbalanced urbanisation witnessed the increasing role of expanding mega-cities and, in terms of economic development, the market-driven process, which is common in developing countries. By 1994, the three city regions of Shanghai, Beijing and Guangzhou, covering only 2 per cent of the country's total land area and accommodating just 10 per cent of the total population, together formed some 50 per cent of the country's urban population and contributed 27 per cent to the country's total GDP;[4] this urban trend is recently becoming even stronger, spurred by land development.

During the 1990s, large cities with traditional state-owned industrial bases were losing their advantage and jobs to flourishing township enterprises, especially in the SEZs, due to their limited decision-making powers and heavy social burden. The deindustrialisation of urban processes in large cities accelerated. Some saw rapid redevelopment for new housing, commerce and offices in the inner-city areas, especially after the land-market reforms of 1992. Many big cities began to develop more advanced capital- and technology-intensive service industries, for example the establishment of financial districts (including Pudong in Shanghai and Jinrongjie in Beijing) and aircraft manufacturing in Shanghai.

China's contemporary urbanisation is tied to the financial reforms that gradually restructured the nation's social wealth distribution pattern.[5] While both private enterprises and individuals were gaining more (81 per cent in 2000, up from 66 per cent in 1970), the state weighed less in national income (19 per cent in 2000 down from 34 per cent in 1970).

Decentralisation in urban development has enabled existing social groups to localise resources that they already possessed, including land, infrastructure, property, location, accessibility to power and money, and so on, according to their existing social, economic and political status. Therefore, as soon as the SEZ policies were issued, almost every city and every town set up its own localised SEZ in order to attract investment.

Changing patterns in the distribution of wealth and the increasing role of government enterprises and the private sector consequently weakened the planning power of governments at all levels and encouraged uncoordinated urban developments, challenging the existing order of the city in many senses. The rise of localism and severe urban competition within the same city often caused great waste in resources for repetitive investments. In the PRD, for instance, five major airports have been built within five major cities without coordination or limited air-traffic volumes. Instead of healthy cooperation between cities, serious problems including lack of water, traffic congestion, housing pressures and historic conservation are the consequences that competing cities now have to face.

Taking Beijing as an example, the location of the Central Business District (CBD) has long been part of the city's masterplan. However, after the property market was opened up in 1992, the East and West City Districts competed to attract investments in office space by proposing CBDs under their own jurisdiction, regardless of the serious consequences, particularly in terms of traffic congestion. Later the Haidan and Fengtai districts of Beijing also planned their own kind of CBDs in the city.

Existing patterns in land-use ownership and the absence of any unified land market made Chinese planning coordination powerless. In practice, anarchistic urban landscapes were created, as shown by the 3,000 high-rise buildings in the centre of 1990s Shanghai.

The enormous potential profits in China's property market have made real estate a rapidly expanding sector since 1992, making it

The chaotic high-rise buildings of Shanghai mixed with the old city fabric that has rapidly been redeveloped over the past 10 years.

the major source of local governments' tax revenues. Decentralised economic powers have caused uncontrolled land development both within and beyond urban areas. At the same time, each new local government tends to designate a new area for duplicated development even if there may have been low actual usage of previous similar developments or some lands still available, as witnessed in many cases of industrial parks and the large volume of empty office buildings in newly developed areas. Since the 1980s there has been a whole series of planning zones marketed under endless new development types such as SEZs, industrial zones, CBDs, high-tech development zones, eco-towns, cultural industry parks, new townships and even themed new cities. In reality, however, most of these new development zones end up simply as plain real-estate development.

Consumerism is another major social aspect of the reform and urbanisation process. With a widening income gap, China has witnessed a rise of an urban middle class that has increasingly become the leading force for consumption, accelerating the nation's consumer power in the world. Housing, cars, leisure, travel and fashion are the key items of the new consumer society,[6] and form the core sociocultural dimensions of China's urban development from massive shopping malls, bar areas, theme parks and suburban housing estates to fantasy architectural and urban expressions.

In the last few years, with increasing environmental and social pressures among others, the Chinese government has gradually realised the importance of a 'harmonious' development model if the sustainability and long-term interests of the country are to be guaranteed. In urbanisation terms, this suggests less rapid development and increased efforts in social developments, including investment in low-income housing, community services and public transport. This may hopefully provide an opportunity for a more balanced, quality-oriented urbanisation process, but it is by no means an easy target given the forecast of vast numbers moving to the cities and general environmental constraints. ∆

Oriental Plaza is a recent major office development in central Beijing, close to the Forbidden City.

Notes

1. Hu Angang and Wang Zhaoguang, *Report on China's Regional Differentiations*, Liaoning People's Publishing House (Shenyang), 1995.
2. Lu Dadao et al, *Annual Report on China's Regional Development – 1999*, Shangwu Publishing House , 1999.
3. Huang Ping (ed), *Away from Home for Survival: A Sociological Examination of Rural Labour in Non-Rural Sectors*, Yunnan People's Publishing House (Kunming), 1997.
4. Gao Ruxi and Luo Mingyi, *The Economic Development of City Regions in China*, Yunnan University Press (Kunming), 1998.
5. Zhang Jie, 'A Theoretical framework for China's current urban developments', Chinese Academy of Social Sciences (CASS) and Swedish Council for Planning and Coordination of Research (FM) joint seminar on 'Globalization and its impacts on Chinese and Swedish society', Beijing Conference, 6–10 October, 1997.
6. Li Peilin (ed), *Report on Social Stratification in Contemporary China*, Liaoning People's Publishing House (Shenyang), 1995.

Decentralised economic powers have caused uncontrolled land development both within and beyond urban areas.

The SOHO residential redevelopment of a former industrial site in Beijing.

Leaving Utopian China

Until the late 20th century, China was a rural society with an agrarian economy and had little experience of the urban. This elevated the city in the collective imagination to a miraculous mirage – a utopian vision. **Zhou Rong**, Associate Professor at Tsinghua University School of Architecture, Beijing, and Assistant Mayor of Shuozhou, describes how China has learned, earned, consumed and ultimately suffered from this idealisation of the urban.

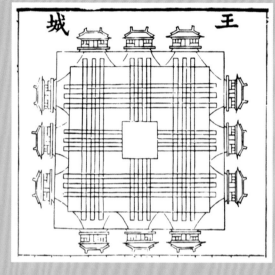

Map of the imperial capital city of the Zhou dynasty (9th century–256 BC) – the classical model of an ideal Chinese city. From *Illustrations of the Rites of Zhou and the Book of Etiquette and Ceremonies, and the Book of Rites,* by Nie Chongyi (Song dynasty).

Zhou Rong and Cheng Ying, *Shangjing Story*, 2006.
In this artwork, Beijing's four modern landmark buildings are treated like a utopian banquet.

Digital rendering of a PowerPoint city. Most visualisations of urban development take the form of PowerPoint presentations of digital imagery to impress governments and property developers.

Utopian urbanisation in China should be seen in the present tense rather than as a distant ideal. If the process of urbanisation can be understood as a procedure of organising all the urban resources more efficiently, the current mode in contemporary Chinese cities is undoubtedly utopian. This brings an anti-experiential, antihistorical, arbitrary, purified, slick-city model to the world, which is at the same time a miracle and a mirage.

Learning from Utopia

To understand contemporary Chinese 'utopian cities', it is important to comprehend the basic situation that the Chinese city governments faced in the initial years of intense urbanisation. Over the past thousand years, China had very little experience of being a city-based society compared to its experience of being a rural society with an agrarian economy. The communist government had almost no experience of dealing with urban issues when it took over mainland China in 1949. After 30 years of isolation from the West, the Chinese government had to initiate its modern urbanisation process, lacking experience and workable concepts. Utopian models were, therefore, the only choice the government had at the time.

The utopian urban model in China comes from three historical sources: the native cultural tradition that perceives the Chinese city as a symbol of ritual and order; imported Soviet ideology that views the city as an opportunity to show off the advantages of socialism; and the distorted modern notion of the urban, adopted from Hong Kong, that regards the city as a showcase for modernisation. In Chinese history, most newly formed dynasties would burn down the old palaces as soon as they took over the country, and build a brand-new city to set out the new order of the new ruler. The phenomenon of the tabula rasa in newly built contemporary Chinese cities shows a similar ambition to erase old affections and establish an unassailable new order.

Earning from Utopia

Since the late 1970s and the widespread collapse of communist beliefs in China, the government has been eager to produce a system of new ideals – a utopian city myth – to reinforce its rule. Utopian cities bring new hope and faith to the common people. In fact, the utopian city has become the collective Chinese dream in the past 15 years, through the promotional propaganda and mega-events of central and local administration aimed at rapid and vast-scale economic developments, especially in building a new society through brand-new or revamped cities (for example, 'New Beijing' for the Olympics).

In the name of city development, the social benefits of the city originally endowed to the people have been 'robbed' by the administrative bureaucracies and capital-class who are undertaking development for the sake of commercial profit. Under the umbrella of utopian cities, the wealthy and poor are seriously polarised by the uneven distribution and control of urban resources.

Consuming from Utopia

The contemporary Chinese urban utopia is a tourist utopia – a superficial utopian image of entertainment for fast consumption. Under the grand halo of utopian cities are hidden urban landscapes of poverty and slums in vast urban villages, especially in rapidly growing cities such as Shenzhen and Guangzhou. However, the appeal of these idealised visions perpetuates the overwhelming Chinese dream. In so doing, the whole world also becomes a consumer of the Chinese utopian city vision.

Thus, to satisfy the consumer appetite for Chinese utopian visions, nearly every city has produced a visual orgy of its utopian futures from digital renderings and animations of the city's future planning, whether practical or not. Impressive digital fly-throughs are commissioned by most city administrations as marketing road shows to attract investment, and are gradually being seen overseas, as in the recent 'China Design Now' exhibition at the V&A in London. These modern utopian visions always include skyscrapers, megastructures, superwide roads, and superscale real-estate development projects. City governments consider these real achievements for political gain, rather than mere marketing. Digital renderings of city utopias are presented

«Строим», В. Кулагиной.
Издание «Известий ЦИК СССР и ВЦИК» Москва,
1929 г.

via PowerPoint as clean picture-perfect imagery for marketing purposes to both government institutions and the general public. Such synthesised visions tend to be generic and repetitive.

Suffering from Utopia

The contemporary Chinese utopian city deceives not only the viewer, but also those involved in its realisation. City governments really believe in the illusion of the utopian city and are set on achieving it at any cost. The discrepancy between the utopian concept and real life is becoming more problematic and irresolvable.

Two well-known recent events revealed the fragility of the Chinese utopian dream. An officer for the city administration in Beijing was killed by a pedlar when he attempted to confiscate the vendor's booth because the city has a zero-tolerance approach to untidiness. In the end, the official was proclaimed a 'martyr' by the city government. The second story is that of the owner of a 'nail house' (the last house standing on a demolition site) in Chongqing who fought against the city government and real-estate developer for months and finally won the court case (such famous public court cases between inhabitants who refuse to move, demanding fair compensation, and local city governments have in the past few years appeared frequently in the media). The utopian 'martyr' and the anti-utopia hero here both mirror the current state of urban delusion.

Leaving Utopia

Chinese utopian cities may have now almost exhausted their initial energy. Utopian-driven development systems are suffocating under the vigour of the city, just as the original richness and diversity of cities seemed to be threatened by the new forces of urbanisation. Potential resistance to established utopian developments is already appearing in some well-developed Chinese cities. This can be seen in the case of self-organised urban areas in Beijing, such as San Li Tun Pub Street, Gui Jie Restaurant Street, the Shi Cha Hai Leisure Area and Dashanzi Art District, where diversity, cultural interest, personal pleasure and community enchantment with urban life has flourished within a short time, even in the midst of the monotonous fabric of previous urban utopias. Hope may be on the horizon: China's departure from utopia being imminent. ◭

The Garbage Collector Village near Beijing's East 4th Ring Road. In the background is a high-end housing project.

Potential resistance to established utopian developments is already appearing in some well-developed Chinese cities.

Soviet utopia artwork: *We are Building,* by Valentina Kulagina, 1929.

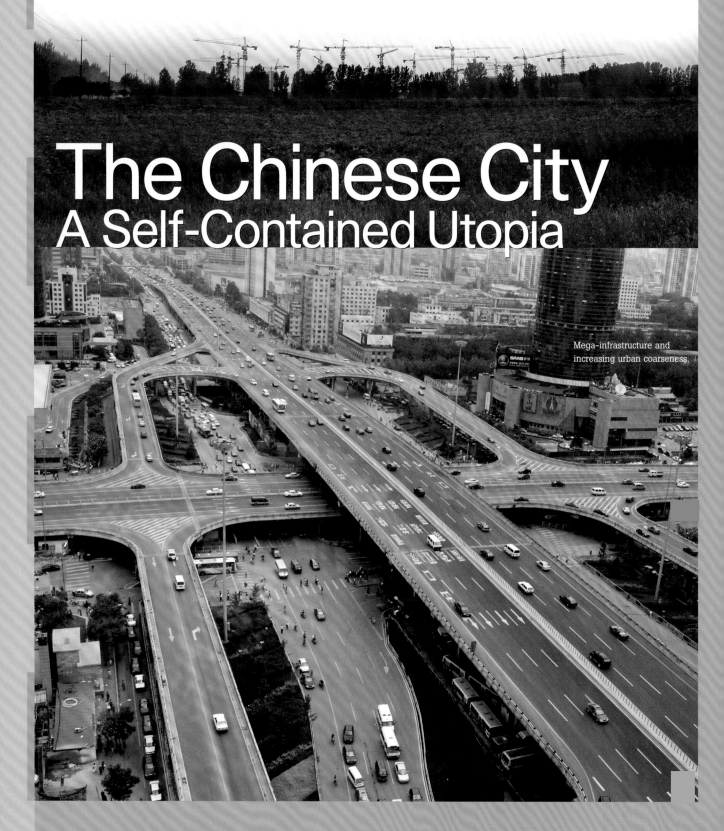

Rapid peripheral growth north of Beijing.

The Chinese City
A Self-Contained Utopia

Mega-infrastructure and increasing urban coarseness.

Could the utopian ideal of building a tabula rasa city from scratch be slipping away? **Neville Mars,** Director of the Dynamic City Foundation (DCF), Beijing, highlights how in the last decade development has become focused on the periphery of existing metropolises. Fuelled by the aspirant middle classes' inexorable appetite for settling in modern cities, urbanisation is manifesting itself in 'self-contained utopias': walled-off, slick cities that are dormitory, satellite towns rather than independent urban settlements.

The success of contemporary Chinese cities, built in a single generation, was founded upon an almost utopian quality: a dreamscape that only seemed to get better. For the people living this dream, confronted with so much progress, questioning the future seemed senseless. Progress was never intended to be utopian. For the first time ideological rhetoric was replaced by market pragmatism to realise a new Chinese dream: the new middle class settling into modern cities.

With migration to cities driving global urbanisation, this should also be the global dream. However, in China the crudest form of 20th-century modernity is on offer, at a time when the developed world has come to acknowledge its shortcomings. Mesmerised by new-found consumerism, the emerging middle class looks ahead and marches on. The central government, on the other hand, is increasingly aware that a passionate adoption of Western-style progress can no longer suffice. There are imminent dangers looming, in perfect symmetry: the exclusion of the bulk of China's citizens from much of the progress and the presentation of the poorest with the bill for rampant environmental degradation; all contemporary shortcomings are mirrored directly to

The typological shift from *hutong* (a narrow street lined by traditional courtyard residences) to high-rise.

Demolition and resurrection in the heart of Shanghai.

become outstanding objectives for the future. China now boasts radical schemes for (almost) all aspects of society, ranging from welfare to technological innovation, encompassing environmental sustainability and moon landings.

Fluctuation between the big hazards and big hopes is not new. Responding to crisis has been key to China's success. Since the inception of reform in 1978, every successive wave of change has come out of a predicament posed by disaster. Decreasing state funding and fewer direct subsidies from central government, along with marketisation, pushed local governments close to bankruptcy in the early 1980s. However, in the mid-1980s the first land reforms were put in place to allow local governments to lease and develop areas under their jurisdiction, unlocking the world's most rampant building frenzy.

Employed as a political tool, urbanisation has become increasingly streamlined, pragmatic and often relentless. The Maoist dream of collective ownership is auctioned off in bits. The state launches its mega-projects, while solo developers sear holes into the once communal urban carpet to create pristine patches for hassle-free privatisation. Plot-by-plot urbanisation facilitates a controlled unravelling of 'capitalism with Chinese characteristics' – a hybrid that can realise vast projects such as the Olympics, and indeed the overhaul of Beijing itself, at lightning speeds because it can expedite any procedure, switching freely between public and private operations.

The current political climate in China is geared towards the construction of new cities. This is central to economic development and long-term stability. However, after a rapid surge of an average of 23 brand-new cities created annually during the 1980s and 1990s, suddenly, from 1998, no new cities were recorded. The birth of a city is a matter of policies. Urbanisation is a goal to be attained, but preferably without the disadvantage of conceding the granting of expensive city benefits or losing state control. However, policies were easily adapted, and outside of the official regulations around a hundred new towns of substantial size have mushroomed across China in the last decade, in the form of mining towns, tourist towns, suburban enclaves, factory villages, themed and concept towns, and military settlements (see Jiang Jun's and Kuang Xiaoming's article in this issue on the taxonomy of Chinese cities – pp 16–21).

Slick Cities

Increasingly these new urban settlements are 'slick cities' – clean residential strongholds fortified against their muddled surroundings. The walled-off neighbourhoods that have dominated Beijing, consisting of extruded versions of the dormitory typology, are now spreading across the nation. Compared to their industrial predecessors, slick cities look and feel smooth. But there is a price to pay. They are by nature static. Their walled-off space is unyielding to change. Exploded in size, their architecture negates the necessity for planning beyond connecting technocratic transit arteries. Apprehension has entered the planning domain. Congested points are crowd-managed with the insertion of ever larger plazas and walkways. Pedestrian traffic and cars alike hurtle through voids and highways. Congestion is inevitable; human encounters unlikely. Planning has become the practice of moving people out and voids in. The fabric of the slick city is stretched apart; the expansion and fragmentation of the city accelerates. Urban and suburban begin to blur.

China's slick cities are loathed but also loved, both at home and abroad. European architects condemn their soulless spaces, while Africa, the Middle East and India herald their scale, speed and rationalised shine. The Mayor of Mumbai hopes to make Mumbai (currently a metropolis composed of 6 per cent slums) into a city just like Shanghai by 2010 (as quoted in the *South China Morning Post* in 2007). For millennia, the Chinese Empire has used cities as a means to safeguard

'Brickification': rural *in situ* urbanisation.

Leisure – the new dominant urban ingredient.

A middle-class gated community.

the vast expanse of its rule, as perfect beacons of power. Meticulously designed and walled off in city quadrants with little regard for public space, they could be copied efficiently *en masse*. These were the first slick cities.

City Organics

Any conventional notion of planning will be inadequate when urbanisation occurs faster than planners can map, driven by constructions at both ends of the urban spectrum: the macro-planned and the micro-organic. The urban designer is presented with a fraught dilemma – to pursue the clean modernity of the economic miracle or to stimulate the human vibrancy of Chinese entrepreneurialism. Both forms fear each other, yet feed off each other. While we deliberate, aggregated projects grow the urban landscape in the form of more 'market-driven unintentional development', or MUD.

MUD formations fracture the beliefs in both the grass-roots city and the orchestrated landscape. At street level, China's new urban realms look perfectly micro-planned, while the same polished island developments at the scale of the metropolis merge together to evolve macro-organic systems.

The building blocks of China's cities are often designed in days; the ensuing MUD configurations then fixed for decades. Inelasticity of urban growth patterns demands that development equips itself with long-term flexible frameworks. Demolishing and then reconstructing the built environment every generation is totally unsustainable for China.

Midway

The reality is that China is now halfway done; 2008 marks the 30th anniversary of the introduction of China's Open Door Policy and subsequent economic rise. If current growth rates continue, in a further 30 years China's GDP will overtake that of the US, including the shift in employment from primary to tertiary industries and the move from rural to predominantly urban settlements.

Other forms of spatial production have evolved as rural China is also halfway done. Here, too, fear motivates planning. Millions of rural migrants are still barred from permanently settling in cities, and eventually go back to the countryside. Distrust of slums and ex-farmer communities has kept China's citizen (*hukou*) registration system in place. Yet this division between people with urban or rural status is increasingly outdated by the blurred spatial conditions it produces. Planning policies intended to stimulate modern centres are effectively urbanising China outside of the cities when the migrant workers return to their villages and build new and large homes for their families with savings earned in the cities, or redevelop the villages with more urbanised facilities, encouraging the next wave of villagers to relocate to the cities for work.

Parallel Worlds

Though propagating massive utopian schemes and extreme projects at the periphery, the Central Communist Party (CCP) centres its trust in the future on the growing middle class. The ideal 'harmonious society' policies projected on to the future are carried out with each producer turned consumer. However, as China's economic reforms unfold, the tendency to produce MUD formations accelerates the grip that the urban configuration has on Chinese society. The utopian dream to design the city or society from scratch slips away.

The urban Chinese dream is at odds with the CCP's grip on power. Widespread middle-class urbanisation jars

'Eurostyle': currently one of the popular architectural flavours.

Augmenting contrasts in downtown Shanghai.

against centralised control. Exclusivity clashes with the harmonious society. Ultimately, the design of a society contradicts the empowerment of the individual. Building cities will shape China's society, but a modern society cannot be shaped by city building alone. The rigid structure of the self-contained city as a tool of control is challenged by two distinctly dynamic forces: the free market and the population masses. Unaddressed, urbanisation will continue to generate conflicting realities – a discord at the heart of the socialist market hybrid that resonates through China's bid for progress. China is dreaming up parallel worlds, and building a globally connected fortress. Unwittingly, the new middle class may begin to unlock this fortress. ◬

The 'People's City'

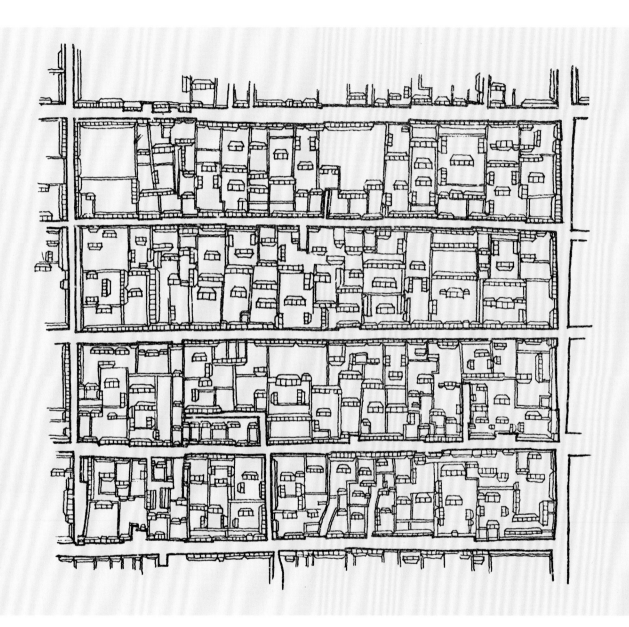

The mid-20th-century communist ideal was for cities that were 'of the people, by the people and for the people'. **Wang Jun,** an editor at *Outlook Weekly* magazine and author of a best-selling book on the planning of Beijing, describes how the ambition to accommodate public life in urban space is a relatively modern phenomenon that goes against the grain of a long tradition of landownership in China. Given this background, can the original notion of the 'People's City' ultimately survive the current wave of property privatisation?

More than 2,000 years ago during the Spring and Autumn (770–476 BC) and Warring States (476–221 BC) periods, China's landownership system underwent a fundamental change from one in which the land was owned exclusively by the king. During the Spring and Autumn period, the king's land began to be privatised, and the duke states began to recognise and legalise the new private ownership of the land. Such privatisation spread rapidly during the Warring States period, and along with this came the introduction of taxation on the land. The Qin state (one of the warring states under the Zhou dynasty) witnessed the most thoroughgoing land privatisation, and thanks to the wealth it accumulated from this and the subsequent land taxation, it became the richest and most powerful of all the seven warring states, which eventually enabled it to unify China in 221 BC. From that time onwards, until about a thousand years ago, neighbourhoods in China's cities were encircled by walls, and streets were not permitted to be used for commercial purposes. Commercial activities took place only at officially designated marketplaces. It was only later, during the Northern Song dynasty (AD 960–1127), that the walls were removed by the people and city streets began to bustle with commerce and public life. The same period witnessed the introduction of an urban property tax levied according to location and prosperity.

Privatisation and taxation of the land has a long tradition in Chinese society. It was, however, a tradition that was challenged during the construction of the 'People's City' ideal in the latter half of the 20th century, following the founding of the People's Republic of China in 1949. The new communist government wished for socialist cities to serve the people, cities 'of the people, by the people and for the people'.

The logic of the People's City generated from many people's belief after 1949 in the 'Planned Economy combined with Land Nationalisation belonging to the Country = Social Welfare State'. Such ideological trends originated in the West, and can first be seen in Sir Thomas More's Utopia of 1516, which proclaimed that private ownership of property was the source of evil in society. More's portrayal of a utopian society consisted of a public-ownership system with more than enough materials and resources to be assigned for everyone to share. However, this utopian situation has remained unattainable, and is almost inconceivable in our modern-day world.

Hutongs (narrow streets lined by traditional courtyard residences) in Beijing during the Qing dynasty (1644–1911). Such lanes crossing the neighbourhoods could be used by communities and also by the city. This urban form of ancient China began to take shape from the Northern Song dynasty (960–1127) onwards. (From Atlas of Beijing in the Reign of Qianlong, AD 1750, published by the Beijing Yanshan Publishing House, 1997.)

Flourishing commerce along the streets of Bianliang, the capital of the Northern Song dynasty (960–1127), after the removal of the walls that encircled the neighbourhoods. The hand-painted scroll, the Qing Ming Shang He Tu by Zhang Zeduan, one of the Song dynasty's greatest artists, shows a riverside scene during the Qing-Ming Festival.

A slogan painted on the wall of a courtyard in Dong Cheng District, Beijing, during the Cultural Revolution (1966–76) paying tribute to Mao Zedong (Chairman Mao) with the words 'Great leader, Great teacher'.

The Chinese character *Chai* (demolition) painted on the wall of an old house in Beijing in 2007 – a sign that the house will soon be torn down.

The entrance of the Ministry of Construction. The ministry has its own collective-living compound – *dayuan* ('gated community') – which is located behind the office building. The *dayuan* courtyard includes its own restaurants and public bathhouse.

A Beijing *hutong* with more than 700 years of history being torn down in 2002.

During the first half of the 20th century, after the Great Depression and two world wars, searching for changes to the Old order became a global trend. Left-wing intellectuals who aspired to a planned economy and the state ownership of land had a profound impact on the development of cities. In 1944 British economist FA Hayek pointed out in *The Road to Serfdom*[1] that the planned welfare state was not a fight for individual freedom, but a step towards autocracy. However, after 1949 the majority of Chinese people believed that a great era of the People's City was coming, with highly centralised planning and state ownership, and for 30 years after the formation of the People's Republic of China such policies were indeed imposed.

This model allowed the Chinese government to carry out rapid industrialisation of the country during the 1950s and 1960s. However, in cities, the policies caused grave contradictions: private land and housing was constantly confiscated and nationalised by the state, hence the amount of property taxation from the land kept decreasing, meaning that most cities' tax income could not meet the financial needs of public service provision. At this point, from the beginning of the 1950s, China's urban public services and utilities began to be provided by state-owned administrative/employment units called *danwei* that managed urban collective-living compounds. The compounds covered large tracts of the city's land and were encircled by walls with a few gated entrances, forming so-called *dayuan*, or 'gated communities'. Inside such communities were office and residential areas, and communal services (including kindergartens, hospitals, eateries, grocery shops and so on), combining to resemble mini-cities, whose forms were similar to China's walled cities of a thousand years ago. Outside the walled compounds, however, the urban space was another concern, lacking in public services including infrastructure; even though the government's motto was 'to serve the people', its financial situation (with less tax from property, and relying on tax only from industrial production and commercial businesses) meant it could not fulfil even basic needs.

In 1929, the American urbanist Clarence Perry had proposed the neighbourhood-unit concept of planning, in which self-contained residential areas were bounded by major streets, with shops at the intersections and a school in the middle.[2] The separation of traffic and residential areas was further expounded in 1942 by the assistant traffic commissioner for London, Sir Herbert Alker Tripp, in his influential *Town Planning and Road Traffic*.[3] The big compounds in Chinese cities followed these ideas, which advocated the expansion of urban blocks for car transportation, favouring large gated communities. This led to a situation whereby cities were designed for cars rather than for human beings.

The Planned Economy (1949–78) disregarded normative values: social wealth, for instance, no longer related to true values, but was determined by government administration units and their 'importance'. Each unit's importance depended on their power and rank. Therefore wealth was no longer distributed equally – a person with 'high power' would have more social wealth – and this system also exposed the negative side of the People's City.

People's commune apartments in Xi Cheng District, Beijing. Beijing's municipal government built three people's commune apartment blocks in 1959, the year of the 10th anniversary of the People's Republic of China. Initially all apartments were without kitchens, and families had no choice but to go to public eateries within the communes to dine. However, with the failure of this new yet inconvenient lifestyle, in 1961 the central government revoked the policy of promoting such public eateries and they were changed into public kitchens available to residents.

In 1978, China began to reform and Open Door (open-market) mechanisms were introduced. However, the poor financial condition of cities did not recover immediately. In 1982, China's revised Constitution stipulated that all the urban land should be repossessed by the state (all land in China is ultimately owned by the state), and later, in 1988, it adopted Hong Kong's land policy whereby local governments released leased land through the transfer of land-rights as a form of financial power, these rights being sold to developers. Thus the city's income then came not only from industrial and commercial tax, but also from the selling of leased land-rights. This initiated the government-led redevelopment of old cities, involving the large-scale demolition of housing and the relocation of residents after such land was repossessed by the state. In 1998, China's housing system reforms began to focus more on privatisation, putting a stop to the previous direct assignment to residents from government or employers of actual housing, and replacing this with subsidies and bank loans to buy their own homes. Many relocated residents quickly bought new houses, which resulted in economic growth. However, the loans and subsidies were often not enough to buy a new house, giving rise to further contradictions. Thus as more cities were redeveloped in this way, the gap between rich and poor increased. Though city governments made considerable financial income from selling land, this only encouraged them to demolish more old houses to seize more land.

All of these contradictions were the results of the changes in the landownership system since 1949. The People's City ideal had aspired to social welfare, and people believed a state-owned land system would make it a reality. However, the 1944 reform of the tax system, which meant that local governments and central government shared the revenue from property taxes, greatly lessened public service provisions in the cities, and resulted in the loss of important means of adjusting the gap between rich and poor. After private housing was introduced within China in 1998, 145 cities were still without an affordable housing system, and out of 4 million households promised subsidised housing by the government, only 268,000 had received it by the end of 2006. It has been a big headache for Chinese cities that their investment in public services cannot recoup sufficient profits to sustain them.

Today, more than 80 per cent of urban housing in China is privately owned. The ownership of a house is a household's greatest financial asset, and there is an ever stronger sense of community participation among house owners. By 2004, there had already been 30,000 registered complaints to the Ministry of Construction, which oversaw urban residents' relocation. In 2007, China passed a landmark property law to protect residents' private property rights, and new 'property taxes' are now being planned. The same year, the 17th National Congress of the Communist Party of China proposed revising the political system to encourage the 'well-ordered' participation of residents and promote autonomy in communities. However, with the state-owned land system still functioning, whether or not these reforms will allow the People's City to return to its fundamental meaning remains to be seen. ∆

Notes
1. FA Hayek, *The Road to Serfdom*, Routledge (London), 1944.
2. CA Perry, 'The neighborhood unit', in T Adams (ed), *Neighborhood and Community Planning, Regional Plan of New York and the Environs*, Vol VII, New York Regional Plan Association (New York), 1929.
3. HA Tripp, *Town Planning and Road Traffic*, Edward Arnold (London), 1942.

An old neighbourhood street in Shanghai showing the vibrant street life in 2003.

Street Life and the 'People's City'

Could large-scale urban development and an erosion of rights to public space prove the death knoll for China's vibrant street life? **Shi Jian**, Planning Director of ISreading Culture in Beijing, looks at the tradition of Chinese street culture and how it is currently shifting and reinventing itself for new urban contexts.

Since 1949, the spatial-urban movement of the 'People's City' has been undertaken by the Chinese government at an unprecedented scale. During this period, China's total population has more than doubled, and its urban populations have also doubled. The subsequent loss of credence of the word 'People' in relation to the rapid urbanisation of China, and the limited investment in public space, have pointed to the failure of this movement. In the new market economy, 'People' have become rootless consumers of urban living space, subjected to omnipresent political, administrative and commercial powers. This has caused the erosion of rights to public space and a lack of community vitality on the street. In the upheaval of urban space that has come about with the construction of new cities and large-scale real-estate development, the creation of new modes of public space for people's participation has remained a repressed desire.

The Chinese urban 'street' here can be defined as the 'street culture' of a traditional city in the context of the contemporary city, where streets are the public space between residential spaces and administrative-commercial spaces, making an important contribution to the charm and character of a community and the city. To resurrect the street space it is necessary to revive the vital social institutions of the city, such as street markets, community facilities, arts spaces, temples, schools and parks, and return the public space to the 'People', as described by Di Wang in his book *Street Culture*:

> Ancient China's cities followed rules of traditional building and planning that were particular to the East, such as parallel urban space, holistic planning and rapid building construction (Beijing in the Ming dynasty, for instance, was constructed within 15 years). 'Street culture' was the significant public space that cultivated folk culture, local culture and the vitality of these cities. It existed not only in the streets and lanes (exemplified by Beijing's *hutongs* and Shanghai's *Longtangs*), but also in teahouses, wine parlours and temple fairs. It was a 'place' where urban folk culture was created, gathered and expressed.[1]

In October 1949, the People's Republic of China was declared and founded at the Tiananmen City Gate, north of Tiananmen Square (the world's largest single public space). Since then the word 'People' has frequently been applied to the public

By 2007, rapid redevelopment in Shanghai had destroyed the street fabric.

Shenzhen People's City centre, 2007. Green spaces are not just for beautification, but also tend to isolate pedestrians from public buildings.

Shanghai's Jian An Temple plaza, 2007. Religion, commerce and residential architecture compete and contrast.

An example of traditional street regeneration in Beijing, 2005.

Beijing's 798 Space in Beijing's Dashanzi Art District, 2006.

An old neighbourhood street in Kunming, the capital and political, economic, communications and cultural centre of Yunnan Province, and (right) the city's newly developed commercial centre, 2006.

Heavens Street, Tiananmen Square, Beijing, 2007. Tiananmen Square is the world's largest single urban public space.

spaces of Chinese cities. Almost all the significant parks and squares used for political gatherings, gardens occupied for political festivals, roads habitually used for political marches, and meeting halls occupied for political meetings, were given names with 'People' in them. In the age of 'politics first', before the market economy, public spaces with 'People' in their titles were political spaces controlled by the state. In those hyper-spaces, 'People' had become a word empty of meaning: rather than referring to living 'Man', it evoked the state machine.

In the past few decades, China's 'desire for development' and 'for consumption' was also driven by political methods, carried out within the framework of comprehensive city planning and institutional management. New regulations for commercial/public buildings enhanced the transformation of functional road systems. Dreams of utopia – whether political, traditional or modern – green movements and public facilities, and the over-commercialisation of the structure of the city and of ancient streets ... all these factors have caused the loss of 'street culture' passed down from traditional urban practices.[2]

Moreover, the new hypercommercial districts built in a hurry in the process of high-speed urbanisation have produced isolated urban islands, and the quality of public space has been totally lost. Nowadays mixed-residential gated communities in cities are becoming exceedingly large, and are constructed according to the imagination of inexperienced real-estate developers. These communities have become alien to the natural context of the city, the 'People' are forced to be helpless consumers within closed micro-cities.

I choose to view Chinese cities, especially Beijing, as culturally schizophrenic. On the one hand I am saddened by the fading of its history; on the other hand, I am excited by its change. I record the ancient city that is passing away, and at the same time I appreciate new buildings. I criticise the problems that are rapidly spreading in the city, while I am enjoying the transformation of urban space. The tension between superficial government propaganda and underlying building regulations results in the hopeless struggle of common folk, coexisting with the realities of urban life. This is a game in which self-destruction and restoration of new urban spaces compete,

proceeding without resolution. This could be much more interesting than the actual future of the city, or it may be time for us to declare that the evolution of Chinese urban space and construction should not be totally directed by international models, instead devising its own rules. If so, the most urgent task is to identify, research, criticise and improve these urban spaces.

Facing rapidly spreading, distorted urban spaces in China's cities, the spirit of the 'People' still strives to gradually discover its own reality, by re-creating and managing its own street or public space. The 798 Space in Beijing's Dashanzi Art District, and No 50 Moganshan Road in Shanghai, are art spaces developed out of deserted communist-era factories. These renovated areas are not like SoHo in New York, Hoxton in London or Tacheles in Berlin, which are all intimately connected to the heart of the city. In Chinese cities isolated locations on the periphery do not prevent good publicity and they quickly become special representations of contemporary urban space. The artists' villages of SongZhuang and Caochangdi outside of Beijing are utterly different from related international experiences in public art space, in that they challenge and regenerate the common boundary of suburban and urban territories. ∆

Notes
1. Di Wang, *Street Culture: Chengdu Public Space, Urban Commoners, and Local Politics, 1870–1930*, Stanford University Press/China Renmin University Press (Beijing), 2006.
2. Jane Jacobs' *The Death and Life of Great American Cities* was first published in mainland China in 2005 by Yilin Publishing. It quickly created a great commotion and became a best seller in the academic world. In commemoration of her death, in 2006 Yilin published a special edition that included reviews from several scholars within the country. My own review was as follows: 'In analyzing the American city in reality and an introspection of the fundaments of the modernist scheme, *The Death and Life of Great American Cities* suggested a new and constructive view for the city's renaissance and future. Seeing Jacobs' vivid writing that paralleled us with cities that also embodied mechanisms that were bureaucratic and 'disruptive' for cities such as New York and Chicago, we will discover sympathy for each other. On the other hand, a consciousness of civic concern penetrates the entire novel. However, it was different from the modernist vantage perspective, as the author created an ideal of urban renaissance through details, events, and personal/emotional perspectives. On this the author did not fall in the superficial delusion of the modernist urban planning, but proclaimed a total renaissance and called for depth and vigor in constructing a city.'

The edition also included a review by Wang Jun (see also his article in this issue on pp 44–47): 'The problems suggested in *The Death and Life of Great American Cities* almost totally align with those of China's modern cities and could *rouse the deaf and enlighten the benign*. Today China's urban planning conveys a strong sense of the period before *The Death and Life of Great American Cities* or the era in pre-1961 America where the city's problem was only a problem of material substance and not a problem of society. The key, behind the so-called 'problem of substance', is actually 'non-substance' that returns us to Jane Jacobs' perspective.'

Unknown Urbanity

Towards the Village in the City

The popular portrayal of the Village in the City (ViC) is as a threatened anomaly. On TV and in photojournalism it is most often depicted as a single surviving, washed-up rural community surrounded by a sea of urban high-rises, where ex-farmers use the vestiges of their land-rights to cash in as landlords. Amsterdam-based Japanese architect **Yushi Uehara** contradicts this view by describing how the Vic represents a significant form of 'dynamic resistance created in an exceptional bottom-up process'.

Caiwuwei Village, Shenzhen, Guangdong Province, 2005
Shops filled the ground level of the Caiwuwei ViC, transforming it into a small, socially sustainable environment that supported the lower-income population.

Villagers typically congregated casually in between village blocks to play mah-jong or for family gatherings. With no farms to run, their lives were endless rounds of mah-jong, haircuts and dim sum. They sent their sons to famous American universities in the hope that they would one day become politically influential.

Former site of Caiwuwei Village, 2007
Opposite: The ViC forms a nested autocratic cohabitation system, forming an intriguing autonomy of village authority within the state authority. Caiwuwei ViC was surrounded by the National Theater, bank headquarters, the police headquarters and a popular commercial street. Between 2005 and 2007, Caiwuwei Village was demolished, and in 2008 the Caiwuwei name instead became synonymous with the centre of Shenzhen's financial activities under the flag of the newly built 400-metre (1,312-foot) high International Financial Centre. The image here shows a six-storey villa on the former village site, the owners of which refused to accept the compensation offered by the developer, who plans to build a financial centre in its place.

Upon my first visit to a Village in the City, I saw a dense structure abruptly interrupting the cityscapes of Chinese urbanity. This anomalous fabric consisted of tiny towers, mostly seven floors high, in an extremely compressed layout, as if it were zipped up electronically. The impression was one of human scale, a feeling of place and space that was missing in the surrounding make-believe city. I was told that this settlement had previously been a farming village.
Yushi Uehara, Guangzhou, 2004

The phenomenon of the Village in the City (ViC) is often viewed as part of the urban terrain of erasure and transformation: the structural shift from agrarian life to urbanity. It is perceived as merely a social incident by the majority of Chinese, the downside of today's flourishing China. Yet on the contrary for those who live there, it is a form of dynamic resistance created in an exceptional bottom-up process. This phenomenon exemplifies the difference between bottom-up Chinese urbanisation and that of the conventional top-down approaches imposed elsewhere.

The origin of the ViC phenomenon is anecdotal, marked by the fate of a fishing village called Caiwuwei in Shenzhen. In 1977, its inhabitants found themselves mapped right on to the planned route of the new Hong Kong–Shenzhen railway line. Obviously, Caiwuwei had to make way for it. The village land was relocated and given a new position slightly more to the west of the original location. The rapidly expanding Shenzhen quickly surrounded this newly relocated tiny village, which resulted in further relocation in 1992, rearranging the spontaneous agglomeration into a tight grid. Intriguingly, during this process the village extended its height upwards until it reached the maximum that Chinese urban code permits without the use of elevators.

Providing cheap lodgings in the city centre, ViCs such as Caiwuwei attract migrants, enabling villagers to easily let any available accommodation. From this moment onwards the villagers, who are ex-farmers, become effortlessly rich. With no farms to run, their life is one of an endless round of mah-jong and dim sum. These villagers become, in effect, builders on expanding their homes, landlords on letting their homes and investors through the money they earn.

As Shenzhen swelled like an urban balloon, the assimilated Caiwuwei Village became a compact footprint of urban 'development'; this is how the first Village in the City came about. Since then, ViCs have spread like wildfire, following economic development around China, and Shenzhen now has 192 ViCs containing close to half the entire city population on only 5 per cent of its landmass.

The vitality of the ViC phenomenon is based on historically defined rights and transaction principles concerning land. During the agrarian revolution that lasted between 1949 and 1951, far-reaching land reforms were carried out. Land was confiscated from the large landowners and handed over to one of two new owners: agricultural land went to farmers' collectives and urbanised land reverted to the state. Ever since, 'farmer' or 'citizen' status has been directly linked to the right to possess land – farmers have rights, while urban citizens have none.

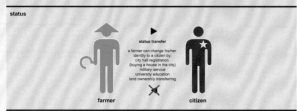

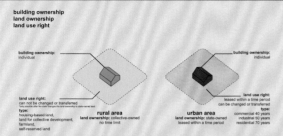

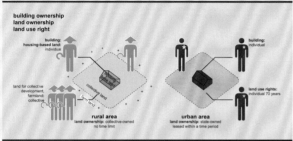

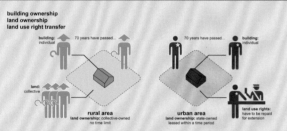

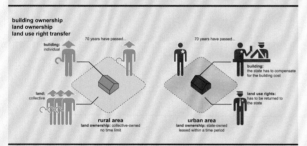

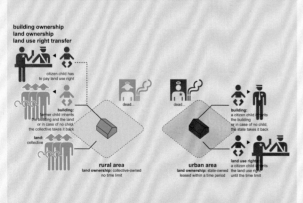

Village in the City diagrams showing the actors involved in ViC creation and the land-use rights mechanism.

In order to make the country operational, Mao Zedong (Chairman Mao) gave farming villages autonomy, with each farmer obtaining an equal share of the harvest. However, one consequence was a substantial drop in productivity.

In 1963, the Private Reserved Land scheme was introduced. This permitted that a small portion of farmland could be privately harvested to boost productivity. After the death of Chairman Mao in 1965, Deng Xiaoping outlined a lease system in farming, the Household Responsibility System, which allowed farmers to lease collective land without payment. This became law implemented later on; this was an immediate success. Farmers started producing what consumers wanted; this, combined with the autonomy of the farming villages, led to the flourishing 'economic miracle'. Interestingly, ViCs grew out of these reforms and Deng's 1970s Open Door Policy and development of Special Economic Zones (SEZs).

There are three groups of 'urban actors' in ViCs who participate in land-use decision-making: local government, the property developer and the end user (migrant workers). The ViCs, once encapsulated, successfully resist being bought out by the city government; they start a nested autocratic cohabitation system, forming an intriguing autonomy of village authorities (in the form of a privatised cooperative governed by villagers that redistributes profits) within the state authority. The villagers' land exploitation rights define their position. However, villagers have only limited years to exploit this loophole. People do die, after all. … In 70 years the villagers' profitable position will have disappeared, since villagers' rights cannot be passed on to their children, so the government is just sitting it out.

In view of the poor city image that the existence of a ViC represents to local government, the current tendency is to press for ViC to be abolished. In the meantime, developers wait and see, because their destruction is so legally complex. In these circumstances, the villagers concentrate on netting the maximum floor–air ratios through the density of their plots. It sounds like a fairy tale, with former farmer cooperative organisations helping their 'colleagues' to upgrade themselves into 'rich citizens'. Meanwhile, the villages' end users, the migrant workers, have no voice at all.

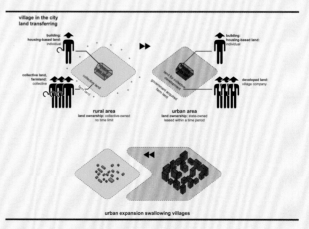

Village in the City diagram showing the land-transferral mechanism and urban expansion.

Shipai Village, Guangzhou, Guangdong Province, 2005
The Shipai Village, spread out over 25 hectares (62 acres) of terrain near the Central Business District in Guangzhou, is a nest for the 40,000-strong floating population of migrant workers. The village is currently planning an RMB400 million redevelopment for China's successful young urban inhabitants.

The emergence of the ViC marked the appearance of capitalism within the communist system. The Chinese constitution guarantees the ownership of collective ground of the villages, even in cities. The Shipai villagers thus opened their enlarged houses to migrant populations and quickly began to collect rents.

Most fascinatingly, this ViC phenomenon is accompanied by a new voice for the urban development of China: the villagers. Before the emergence of this new urban 'actor', China knew only two human profiles: the citizen or the farmer. A villager is now therefore the only property capitalist in China who may own urbanised land. The government pronounced all ViC villagers to be 'citizens' in an attempt to resolve the current contradictions and tensions of urban development. Yet such a decree has provided nothing for farmers to hand down land to their sons. Recent times have seen changes to the landownership law implemented, and in Shenzhen the subsequent combination of political pressure and financial interest finally resulted in the go-ahead for the development of the 400-metre (1,312-foot) high Shenzhen International Financial Centre tower and commercial complex on the Caiwuwei Village site. The demolition of Caiwuwei, the original ViC, took place between 2005 and 2007. The villagers' new apartments will be in three skyscrapers above the new shopping centre.

As urbanisation sweeps over agricultural land, the ViC undergoes four phases of transformation in forming urban settlements: 'freestanding village', 'touching urbanity', 'swallowed by urbanity' and 'erasure'. Under this, a three-way battle over power to rule land ensues. On the basis of the research conducted at the Berlage Institute in 2005, I have reconstructed an academic understanding on the ViC and formed 25 urban actions to describe the process of ViC evolution.[1] Following are some of the primary stages of activity in ViCs:

Extrusion: The villagers 'extrude' their house in order to achieve a profit. The farmer sets his sights on the expanding city and extrudes his home just before the construction of infrastructure. Extrusion also often occurs when a farmer aims to optimise rents to meet the demand for accommodation from the floating population of migrant workers.

Hospitality: The ground-floor areas are often rented out to house small commercial activities, which transform the ViC into a more self-sustainable urban unit servicing the surrounding city.

Neighbourhoods: The ViC installs temples, schools and crèches that enable the floating population to become an even more productive labour force.

Implosion: After the purchase of the farmland, the villager inserts houses for new family members in the small open terrains. This consequentially increases the overall density of the whole ViC.

Education: The now-wealthy businessmen-villagers send their children to Western universities, in the hope they will develop skills to become politically influential.

Visiting the Chinese city, I experience an unreal reality, big simulacra of pure possibility. At the feet of an emerging city of towers, the ViC formations thrive, surmounting this politically flawed urban form on cost-free village land. Offering cheap lodgings for the influx of floating populations, the ViC is a 'saviour of the poor' and a 'sustainer of the rich'; it has achieved a method of land use that interweaves humanity and urbanity, confirming that villagers exercise urbanisation privileges based on market observation, and not on principles of altruism.

The ViC is not about the spatial display of power compared to its neighbouring new residential developments, but provides the greatest opportunity to evolve a new Chinese urban ecology: 'Unknown Urbanity in China.' Δ

Note
1. This research is the result of the year-long second-year research studio 'Village in the City: Unknown Urbanity in China' led by Yushi Uehara during the 2004–05 academic year at the Berlage Institute in Rotterdam, the Netherlands. The project was completed by the following Berlage Institute participants: Yuan-Sheng Chen, Tsai-Her Cheng, Joey Dulyapach, Hideyuki Ishii, Hui-Hsin Liao, Daliana Suryawinata, Taichi Tsuchihashi, Zhang Lu and Ying Zhu.

Urban Villages

Is the Village in the City (ViC) potentially an urban scar or a vibrant community? **Meng Yan**, principal of urban design think tank and architectural firm URBANUS, advocates a design approach to the urban village phenomena that recognises the vitality of the social conditions they provide and how they might, with some intervention from designers, prove a ready-made solution to China's housing problem.

The Village in the City (ViC), as found in the Pearl River Delta (PRD) and other regions of China, has in recent years become a hot academic topic, as exemplified by Yushi Uehara's research at the Berlage Institute in Rotterdam (see pp 52–5) into the mechanisms of this urban type, and that of other researchers at various Chinese universities. URBANUS Architecture & Design regards its involvement with the ViC as one of active participation through architecture, aiming to improve the living conditions of the urban type while maintaining its spatial quality and social structure. This attitude of active engagement reflects URBANUS' effort to search for an innovative architecture through the comprehensive reading of specific urban conditions in today's Chinese cities.

The cause behind the formation of the ViC is simple: a huge amount of agricultural land has been appropriated by cities due to the rapid urbanisation of the past 20 years. However, the unique law protecting villagers' ownership of housing plots in urban districts has remained intact. These urban villages are growing vertically and increasing in density at an even greater rate than the expansion of the surrounding city. Villagers rebuild their original village houses of one or two storeys up to eight storeys in response to increasing land values. Driven by profit and unhindered by a lack of enforceable building regulations, ViCs become a lucrative means of harvesting income for the villager/landlord, and important as the key providers of cheap housing for young migrant workers.

The chaotic appearance of this ex-village type means that aesthetically it is commonly regarded as a scar on the city. Politically, it is perceived as a time bomb because of its high concentration of young migrant workers, poor sanitation, hidden unlawful activities and fire hazards. URBANUS recognises the ViC as an inevitable outcome of the process of urbanisation in China. It could be considered as one of the most common, sometimes dominant, housing typologies in contemporary Chinese cities such as Shenzhen, Guangzhou and other industrial towns (accommodating the majority of the population, but the minority of land occupation). The more people who are able to live a comfortable middle-class lifestyle, the greater number of people on lower incomes, living in these less-than-ideal conditions, are required to service and support the affluent.

China is now at a critical point in time in terms of thinking about how cities might sustain a well-balanced development by absorbing and accommodating the ongoing massive migration of ex-farmers in the coming years. The ViC certainly plays an irreplaceable role in retaining this balance. Compulsory relocation schemes might be able compensate the villager/landlord; however,

URBANUS, Dafen Art Museum, Dafen Village, Shenzhen, Guangdong Province, 2005–06
Dafen Oil Painting Village is in Buji Township, in the Longgang District of Shenzhen. Famous for its replica oil-painting workshops, it exports billions of renminbi (RMB)-worth of paintings globally. URBANUS' museum proposal focuses on reinterpreting the urban and cultural implications of Dafen Oil Painting Village, which has been long considered a peculiar mix of Pop Art, bad taste and commercialism. Can it be a breeding ground for contemporary art and blend with the surrounding urban fabric? Our strategy is to create a hybridised mix of different programmes, like art museums (top image), oil-painting galleries and shops, commercial spaces, rental workshops, and studios under one roof. It creates maximum interaction through the building's public spaces. Exhibition, trade, painting and residences can happen here simultaneously, interwoven into a whole new urban mechanism.

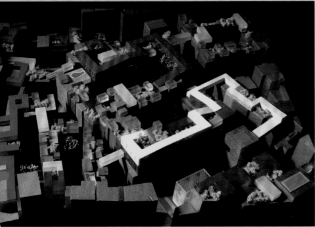

Huang Weiwen, Zhang Jianhui and URBANUS, Proposal for the Dynamic Rehabilitation of Gangxia Village, Shenzhen, Guangdong Province, 2005

In 1996, the 17-hectare (42-acre) Heyuan block had a housing area of 270,000 square metres (2.9 million square feet), which had increased to more than 400,000 square metres (4.3 million square feet) by 2001. Located in the future Central Business District (CBD) in Shenzhen, it faces tremendous rehabilitation pressure. Through partial demolition, infilling, stitching and the addition of public facilities on to the roof, dynamic rehabilitation should be enabled to resolve the existing dense buildings and fragmented public spaces. With better-defined commercial streets, service roads and courtyard-type public spaces, this renovation strategy will dramatically improve the commercial, housing, transportation and community facilities to maintain the existing social structure of the neighbourhood.

these are not realistic solutions for most of the migrant-worker residents relying on the ViC for affordable housing. These villages are not only places to live; they are also basic workplaces for the inhabitants to start small businesses. If this kind of close-knit spatial and social network is destroyed by demolition and enforced relocation, to be replaced by another monolithic high-rise residential compound, then basic communities will vanish from cities.

The unique social and architectural condition of the Village in the City results in vibrant activities; it is a 24-hour mini-city, an urban enclave within the city fabric. Compared to 'well-designed' upper-middle-class gated residential compounds that become isolated islands in the city ignoring the original urban fabric, ViCs form an alternative open structure containing small-scale shopping streets, intimate public places and, above all, opportunities for small businesses. In contrast with the surrounding globalised city, they still retain traces of indigenous creation through the enthusiasm of original villagers and migrants, and demonstrate an extraordinary social vitality and typological diversity in spatial configuration. From an urban point of view, the Village in the City should not be bulldozed.

URBANUS' approach to the Village in the City is pragmatic and viable. ViCs remain the most effective solution today to the housing problems of lower-income communities; hence URBANUS refuses to simply remove them, as certain local governments have done through wholesale demolition. Through two live case studies, Shenzhen's Gangxia Village and Dafen Oil Painting Village, the practice is trying to find a new approach to meet updated regulations and living standards, introducing positive public spaces and accommodation as well as redefining the villages' own local business strategies and strengthening their cultural characteristics. The ViC should be integrated into a socially balanced and sustainable urban development plan, and at the same time maintain local village culture that is beneficial to the entire city. △

Text © 2008 John Wiley & Sons Ltd. Images: pp 56, 58-9 © URBANUS Architecture & Design; p 57 © URBANUS Architecture & Design, photos Chen Jiu

Post-Event Cities

A bird's-eye view of the Beijing Olympic Park showing the 'Birds Nest' and 'Watercube' stadiums in the midst of new real-estate developments and the landscaped central axis.

Planning 'events' such as the 19th-century foreign concessions in the sink ports and the late 20th-century Special Economic Zones (SEZs) have proved an important catalyst for development in China. Professor **Zhi Wenjun**, chief editor of *Time + Architecture* magazine, and architect **Liu Yuyang** look at how the 2008 Beijing Olympics and 2010 Shanghai World Expo are redefining urbanism in China and raising significant questions about the sustainability of the post-event city.

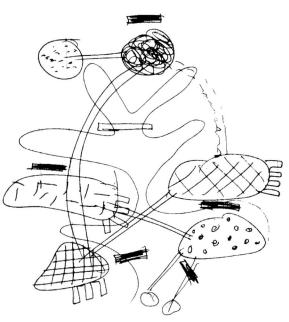

City of Exacerbated Differences (COED) diagram of interconnected and complementary cities in the Pearl River Delta. From Rem Koolhaas et al, *Great Leap Forward*, Taschen GmbH, 2001.

In the not-so-distant past, the 'event-city' referred to the everyday conditions embedded in architecture. In China it is the architecture that is embedded in the event. Consequently, both the nature of the event and that of architecture have changed. Both have become ever more spectacular and highly addictive. Here come the crucial questions: Are these conditions sustainable? If not, how does one cure such addiction?

First off, it is useful to differentiate events in terms of their singularity or recurrence, and in terms of their urban planning and infrastructure strategies. To examine the sustainability question, one may go back to the models of the Special Economic Zone (SEZ) and also look at the City of Exacerbated Differences (COED) for a moment. Both models may be deemed sustainable as they are fundamentally about dynamic changes and responses. SEZ is about the drawing of a singular line, creating a border condition within which flexible policy becomes the most important mechanism for urban growth. The economic reforms initiated by China's paramount leader Deng Xiaoping in the late 1970s not only established Shenzhen, in May 1980, as one of China's first SEZs, but also a series of other coastal cities

such as Xiamen, Zhuhai, Ningbo and Tianjin as additional SEZs, or open-port cities. Due largely to the liberalisation of foreign investment and trade policies, these cities have gained great momentum for growth in areas such as real estate and manufacturing, which fuel the engine for further economic growth domestically.

Back in 1996, a group of Harvard researchers led by Rem Koolhaas came to China's Pearl River Delta (PRD) and worked towards a publication, which has subsequently been published as *Great Leap Forward*.[1] They searched for a valid model to observe the region, which consists of a constellation of small, medium, large and extra-large cities, all competing and affecting one another through political, economic, and infrastructural-architectural means.

The COEDs emerged as one such model to describe a kind of urban growth based on mutually dependent and competitive relationships among the various cities. Negating the traditional notions of harmony, balance, homogeneity, these cities strive for the greatest possible differences among their different parts while collectively maintaining a delicate balance that constantly adjusts to dynamic change, be it economic, social or political. This condition is characteristic of what happened in the PRD when cities like Shenzhen, Dongguan, Guangzhou and Zhuhai suddenly mushroomed into a seemingly chaotic megalopolis as the result of Deng Xiaoping's 1978 economic Open Door Policy.

While China has had a long tradition of centralised control mechanisms, from the central government all the way down to provincial, city and county levels, local governments always found ways to react. Such is the classic Chinese notion of 'policy versus counter-policy'. It is a dynamic, interactive model, as well as a survival model. One observes such dichotomies in both the COED and SEZ models: the establishment of central policies on the one hand, and local responses on the other, forming a dynamic condition of growth by policies as well as counter-policies. Similar conditions can be looked at by comparing examples of 'micro-urbanism' found in other Asian metropolises such as Tokyo or Bangkok, but the PRD remains the most explicit example of

Masterplan of the 2008 Beijing Olympic Park.

Shenzhen COED in the 1990s – a city image modelled on adjacent Hong Kong, but acting as a hub of the rapidly growing COED cities in the Pearl River Delta.

this dynamism which, in all instances, can be described as quasi-organic urban development within an institutional or political framework.

If one goes back in history, one sees that more than a hundred years ago China had a comparable spatial device, the 'concession', which allowed foreign occupation of a smaller piece of land within a larger urban area in exchange for stability and 'controlled' social and cultural experimentation. The citizens within the concession area enjoyed a different set of policies and administration, in a way that is not unlike what we see in the SEZ today. Now, interestingly, many other countries besides China are adopting the SEZ model in an attempt to boost their economies: Malaysia, both North and South Korea, Russia, to name but a few. Thus the SEZ may be seen as one of China's unique political and spatial inventions that has worked for the country in the last 30 years and is now being exported along with all the other Chinese-made products.

So if one considers the COED and SEZ as vernacular Chinese urban conditions and geopolitical inventions, which are spatial and local, their not-so-vernacular counterpart would be the mega-events like the Beijing Olympics and the Shanghai World Expo, which are temporal and global. In a way, events like the Olympics

and the Expo redefine a new way of urbanism in China, creating a new version of 'event city' and hence a certain anxiety about the sustainability of the 'post-event city'. For example, many are now projecting a sharp drop in real-estate markets in Beijing and other cities after the 2008 Olympics, and a greater economic downturn after the 2010 Shanghai Expo. Such anxiety has resulted in the 'addiction' for cities to continue hosting bigger and more events.

The Olympics and Expo are one-off events that demand large-scale construction. They can easily run the risk of providing spectacular architecture and infrastructure that have no future roles in the city. China has experienced a dramatic shift of ideology and policy in dealing with these events. While the Beijing Olympics bolstered the fever for spectacular architecture, symbolised by the Herzog & de Meuron-designed Olympic stadium – nicknamed 'the Bird's Nest' by the Chinese – construction for the Shanghai Expo is being carried out in a different political climate: one that stresses environmental sustainability and social harmony ('Better City Better Life'). The difference is apparent. In Beijing the facilities are mostly placed in a new area outside the current urban centres. In Shanghai, the Expo sites are well within the urban area and right by the Huangpu River where the first of the early 20th-century shipyards built in China are located: this was one of the earliest sites of Chinese industrialisation. Many of the buildings for the Shanghai Expo will utilise existing or renovated old shipyard buildings. At the

The 2nd Shenzhen Biennale of Architecture and Urbanism, 2007. Shenzhen was the first city in China to have an architecture biennale and the event helped regenerate an old industrial district (OCAT) in the city, which now caters to the arts, tourism and residential communities, as well as retaining some light industry.

The Shanghai Expo site under construction on former shipyard land, 2007.

Aerial view of the entire Shanghai Expo development along the Huangpu River at the concept masterplan stage. Shanghai Expo slogan: 'Better City Better Life'.

same time, the boundary between the Expo and the adjacent urban neighbourhoods has been kept porous and interwoven, encouraging post-event integration while maintaining a good balance of existing residential neighbourhoods in the Expo vicinity. The Expo planning strategy may sound absolutely logical and reasonable from the planning point of view, but it was the clarity of the national policy that unified all sides to agree to it.

Another significant change in the case of Shanghai is the simultaneous construction of eight different subway lines. Besides serving visitors during the six-month-long Expo, the new network of subways will drastically transform the way people commute in Shanghai. However, post-Expo is not without its own potential difficulties. For example, some of the exhibition facilities and sites still belong to the state-owned shipbuilding industry. The future of what can be redeveloped on these sites after the Expo remains a contentious issue between the large state-owned enterprise (SOE) and the Shanghai government.

The Shanghai Expo slogan 'An expo to never lower its curtain' proclaims the city's intention to maintain the momentum generated by the event and to continue the urban growth. While it remains to be seen how things will pan out in the next two years, it is possible to speculate a more plausible model: that is, the next stage of event-city, or post-event city, to be based on simultaneous, multiple and recurring events rather than a single mega-event. Recurring events such as the Guangzhou Industrial Trade Expo or the Xiamen Marathon, which draw tens of thousands of exhibitors and buyers in the former case, and equally numerous athletes and spectators in the latter, are valid ways of generating and sustaining urban development. Smaller, more localised events may start to emerge, such as creative industries, art biennales, music

festivals and book fairs. Likewise, architecture as a large, singular, urban spectacle may give way to a multitude of smaller architectural phenomena as a field of urban substance, individually diverse but collective under the institutional framework of sustainability: economic, social, environmental.

More than 40 per cent of the population in China is now living in urban areas, with another estimated 300 million people to be urbanised in the next 20 years. The demand to raise the standard of living for so many people will no doubt be the greatest challenge and opportunity for architecture. Such a demand is based on real needs, not spectacles. Faced with depleting energy resources and increasing environmental pressure, providing for such demands is where Chinese architects, planners and policy makers may contribute most significantly to global society. At the national policy level, the recent Boao Forum for Asia – a regional economic conference hosted by China's president, Hu Jintao, and attended by political and industrial leaders from around the world – focused on the issues of sustainable development and climate change as this year's central theme. Though high on rhetoric without offering substantive implementation tools, the Boao Forum as an event could nevertheless be the right direction for the planning of China's post-event cities to take, in the sense that events become incubators for ideas, policies and actions, not just mere buildings. There may be some utopian optimism in what has been suggested here, but the alternative of not achieving it is too catastrophic to be imagined. ◮

Note
1. Rem Koolhaas, Bernard Chang, Mihai Craciun, Nancy Lin, Yuyang Liu, Katherine Orff and Stephanie Smith, *Great Leap Forward: Harvard Design School Project on the City*, Taschen GmbH, 2002.

Dongtan, China's

An Interview with Peter Head of Arup

Plans for the urban development of Dongtan, an alluvial island in the Yangtze River, close to Shanghai, have captured the world's imagination: Dongtan as a model scheme has become synonymous with the very notion of the 'eco-city', representing China's commitment to sustainability to the world. The Editor of *AD* **Helen Castle** met Peter Head, Director and Head of Global Planning Business at Arup in their London offices, to find out more about their masterplan for the city and the design process behind it.

Arup, Dongtan eco-city, Chongming Island, 2005–
This visualisation of the aerial view of the built city effectively conveys the scale of the development and its incorporation of landscaping and natural wetlands.

Flagship Eco-City

There is no doubt that the concept of the eco-city has now come to maturity: the term 'eco-city' was first coined in print some 20 years ago by the environmental activist Richard Register in his book *Ecocity Berkeley: Building Cities for a Healthy Future*, where he provided an inspirational low-tech guide for making cities ecological.[1] Plans for eco-cities are now proliferating across the world: with Foster + Partners spearheading a design for Masdar City in Abu Dhabi, proposals for eco-cities in the UK and the rest of Europe in the pipeline, and 20 being planned across China alone. None, though, has captured the international media's interest as much as Dongtan. At least a portion of the first demonstrator phase of Dongtan is imminent – it is planned for completion in 2010 in time for the World Expo in Shanghai.

Despite the global realisation of the impact of climate change, it is only in China that building large-scale cities from scratch with minimum resources has become a matter of pressing expediency, as outlined by Herbert Girardet, environmental specialist and author of *Cities People Planet: Urban Development and Climate Change*:[2] 'In China urban growth is fundamentally changing the lives of hundreds of millions of people. So far, this urbanisation process has dramatically increased the country's environmental damage. Dongtan is aiming to show that urbanisation can be a fundamentally sustainable process. Let us trust that the vision of an eco-city powered by renewable energy and free from pollution can become a reality. This is one of the greatest challenges of the 21st century.'[3] In June 2007, the announcement by the Netherlands Environmental Assessment Agency that China's recorded carbon-dioxide emissions for 2006 had surpassed those of the US brought into focus the scale of the environmental crisis in

**Foster + Partners, Masdar Development,
Abu Dhabi, United Arab Emirates, 2007–23**
The alluring set of presentation visuals that has been produced for
Masdar combines the atmosphere of a traditional Arabic city with its
shaded network of internal streets, palm trees and oasis-like pools with
that of a luxury mall.

Foster's design for Masdar is for a sustainable development on the outskirts of
Abu Dhabi that takes the form of a traditional walled city. It aims to achieve a
carbon-neutral and zero-waste community by drawing on vernacular building
knowledge and new technologies. Like Dongtan, it is planned to be the hub of
sustainable research and activity in the region with a new university, the
headquarters for Abu Dhabi's Future Energy Company, Special Economic Zones
and an innovation centre.

China in which mass construction and urbanisation have
played a significant part. It is the soaring demand for coal
to generate electricity and a surge in cement production
that have significantly increased emissions to a level
beyond that of the US: with China producing 6,200
million tonnes of CO_2 in 2006, compared with 5,800
million tonnes from the US.[4]

It is clear that if China is to be able tackle its CO_2
emissions effectively, it must rethink the means by which
it urbanises; between 2007 and 2025, China's urban
population is projected to increase by 261 million
people, so the way in which China accommodates this
burgeoning urban population is critical.[5] Dongtan and
the eco-city initiative in China provide a unique window
of opportunity for sustainable urban design. This flagship
project is being developed by the Shanghai Industrial
Investment Corporation (SIIC), an investment holdings
company owned by the Shanghai Municipal Government
that is one of China's largest property developers; it
operates much like any private company undertaking
commercial deals and has nine overseas regional
headquarters. Arup are under contract with SIIC to
undertake the design of the project. Peter Head, a
director of Arup, who heads up the firm's Global Planning
Business that is overseeing the scheme, explained to me
how they got involved: 'Dongtan was initiated before
Arup's involvement. Shanghai wanted to develop
Chongming Island. The Beijing government were
concerned by this as it presented a threat to the wetland
and ecology of the island. At first the Urban Planning
Institute of Shanghai developed a plan for a scheme

covering 120 square kilometres [46.8 square miles] that they called
eco-city southwest. By August 2005, Arup were engaged.'[6]

In an interview in *Wired* magazine, Alejandro Gutierrez of Arup
describes the alacrity of events in 2004 that led up to the
appointment. Gutierrez, the Chilean-born architect and urban designer,
received a call from some McKinsey consultants in Hong Kong 'who
were putting together a business plan for a big client that wanted to
build a small city on the outskirts of Shanghai. But the land, at the
marshy eastern tip of a massive, mostly undeveloped island at the
mouth of the Yangtze River, was a migratory stop for one of the rarest
birds in the world – the black-faced spoonbill, a gangly white creature
with a long, flat beak. McKinsey wanted to know if the developer, the
Shanghai Industrial Investment Corporation, could bring businesses to
the island without messing up the bird habitat. The consultants
thought Gutierrez's firm could figure it out … He quickly caught a
flight to Shanghai.'[7] Once the project was secured, Arup hired Peter
Head, an eminent bridge specialist, prominent member of the London
Sustainable Development Commission and green guru for London's
Olympic Construction task force, as the firm's first director of planning,
to head up the development. By November 2005 Arup had signed a
contract for four further eco-cities.

The signing ceremony between Arup and SIIC took place at Downing
Street during the state visit of the President of the People's Republic,
Hu Jintao. Since then, the British government has taken a close
interest in the scheme. On the British Prime Minister's visit to
Shanghai on 19 January 2008, Peter Head presented the masterplan
to Gordon Brown at the Shanghai Urban Planning Exhibition Centre
(SUPEC); Brown and the Mayor of Shanghai, Han Zheng, also
witnessed a Memorandum of Understanding (MoU) between SIIC,
Arup, HSBC and Sustainable Development Capital LLP (SDCL),
agreeing to establish a long-term strategic partnership to develop the

funding model for eco-cities in China, a key element of which is the Institute for Sustainability that is to be based in Dongtan.[8] This agreement was to prove an important cornerstone in the UK–China relationship: on the same trip, Brown and Chinese premier Wen Jiabao agreed to boost trade by 50 per cent by 2010 and the British PM also offered China £50 million to help the country tackle climate change. As Head pointed out to me in our discussion, China is setting up similar relationships with other countries such as Singapore, attracting their investment and also tapping into their knowledge of sustainable technologies. (On 18 November 2007, China and Singapore signed a framework agreement for the development of an eco-city project in Tianjin, Northeastern China.)

Prior to Arup's appointment, Dongtan was planned as a dormitory town, a single-use housing development of between 25,000 and 28,000 people. It was very apparent to Arup, though, that Dongtan should not effectively function as a small-scale commuter town. To be ecologically sustainable, it had to be commercially sustainable in order to keep commuting to a minimum. Though it is only planned that in the first phase Dongtan will accommodate a population of up to 5,000, later phases could see the population grow to around 80,000 by 2020 and up to 400,000 by 2050. At present, Arup only control the plan for the 6.5-square-kilometre (2.5-square-mile) start-up area, which is to be completed by 2020, but they should have the masterplan for the whole area of 30 square kilometres (11.7 square miles) completed in about a year. Estimated costs have not been released for the scheme; however, the construction costs

of eco-cities are not anticipated to be significantly different to those of constructing a business-as-usual city. SIIC will bear the costs of the first demonstrator phase of the project and is seeking external investors to fund the further phases.[9]

Arup established the commercial strategy of a Harvard-like model for the city through a socioeconomic study that looked at what jobs might be appropriate. The core element of the strategy is the Dongtan Institute for Sustainability. The ambition is to make it an international centre of excellence for the study of the environment. In the first phase, most jobs are to be associated with teaching, research and providing services for the university, but over time the aim is that spin-off businesses will develop around the institute like they have in Boston around the Harvard and MIT campuses. This is a fairly high-risk strategy, its success being wholly dependent on the success of the institute. It has also led local critics to raise concerns that 'local planners are more concerned with raising the income and standard of living of the region than ensuring ecological development'.[10]

Head describes how in August 2005 Arup initiated their sustainable development work on the project with a workshop involving their client, stakeholders and professionals. It was through this intensive meeting with breakout groups that they came to establish the ambitions of the scheme, which were to run the city on renewable energy, recycle and reuse waste water, protect the wetlands by returning agricultural land to a wetland state creating a 'buffer zone' between the city and the mud flats, and protect air quality by banning fossil-fuelled vehicles (all vehicles have to be battery powered or hydro-cell powered, which makes them quiet as well as non-polluting). The decision to keep petrol-fuelled cars out of the new city informed the organisation of the plan into three villages that meet to form a city centre. All housing is situated within seven minutes' walking distance of public transport. This not only lowers the consumption of energy, but also enables transport to be run on renewable energy. Goods delivery is centred on

Arup, Dongtan eco-city, Chongming Island, 2005–
The city of Dongtan is to be divided into three separate villages that conjoin to form the city centre.

consolidation centres, factored in as part of the infrastructure costs, to enable energy reduction on deliveries, combining commercial logistics with the wider land-use concept.

The form of the masterplan was also informed by the island's social and cultural history. By researching its earlier development, Arup was able to follow relatively recent farming and irrigation channels. Parks are bounded by field edges and field patterns retained. This maintains the relationship with the seasons and natural world. There are 24 parks set in 600 hectares (1,482 acres), each relating to different elements of Chinese culture. For the city to work it is important that the landscape design should resonate culturally.

In order to plan the housing and its urban context, Arup also studied the local street pattern and the way people live in Shanghai: their use of squares, alleys and streets. The microclimate was also important in developing the overall land use. They looked carefully at the orientation of buildings and carried out a detailed study of the orientation of the site. The island is very flat and windy, which is ideal for wind turbines, but also requires a lot of urban planning and the streets to be carefully laid out to prevent them becoming wind tunnels. For the performance specifications that Arup have drawn

On the southeastern tip of Chongming Island in the Yangtze River, Dongtan is across the water from Shanghai.

up for local and international architects designing individual buildings on the site, they studied Chinese standards. Energy consumption, however, as outlined by Head, was an important driver in the design specification for buildings. The use of renewable fuels is to make energy consumption 64 per cent lower than in Shanghai.

The interest of both the Chinese and British governments in the eco-city of Dongtan, and its special status as a demonstration project in both China and across the world, will continue to make it the subject of much media speculation and criticism. Furthermore, Dongtan could hardly be on a more sensitive natural site: its wetlands being one of the most important migratory bird sanctuaries in China. After the rapid development of the masterplan for the city, Arup are now awaiting a final start date from the client, SIIC – with an estimated starting time of the end of 2008 or the beginning of 2009. As Head emphasised to me at the opening of our interview in February 2008: 'The dynamism of the area is so extraordinary that things can change within two to three months.' This makes the final outcome difficult to predict. In the wake of his comment, a wholly unanticipated, human and natural disaster has come in the form of the earthquake that struck Sichuan Province in Western China on 12 May 2008, and has left over 70,000 estimated dead, missing or buried. Though the capital of Sichuan Province, Chengdu, is more than a thousand miles from Shanghai, it is difficult to think that there will be no knock-on effects to funding or construction. The client, however, has given no indication that it is wavering in its commitment to the project, and the high-profile international coverage that this scheme has attracted, as evidence of the Chinese government's commitment to sustainability, will make it difficult, if not impossible, for the Chinese to do a complete U-turn on the scheme. There is no question that Arup's plan would help minimise the environmental impact of development when compared to more conventional development models; certainly, with a bridge-tunnel planned to the mainland and large-scale construction the development will be environmentally disruptive. Expansion is, though, necessary and inevitable in Shanghai: Dongtan is just one of nine new towns planned by the city of Shanghai to relieve overcrowding in a city of more than 20 million people.

At Dongtan, Arup is aiming for high environmental targets: a 60 per cent smaller footprint than in conventional Chinese cities; a 66 per cent reduction in energy demand; to get 40 per cent of the energy supplied from bioenergy; to use 100 per cent renewable energy in buildings and on-site transport; to get landfill waste down by 83 per cent; and to have almost no carbon emissions. The zero carbon emissions goal is one that gets bandied around widely in relation to eco-city schemes – Foster + Partners is also setting out 'to achieve a carbon neutral and zero waste community' with their Masdar development for Abu Dabai.[11] What Arup are clear about, though, is the importance of achieving zero carbon emissions with regard to transport. Dongtan will be effectively a fossil-fuel-free transport zone, only hydrogen-fuel celled and electric private vehicles will be permitted within the city's gates; those driving conventional petrol-fuelled cars will be forced to leave their cars outside Dongtan and take public

Arup's visualisation of the harbour flyover at Dongtan, showing (in the foreground) the bridge-tunnel that is to link Chongming Island to the mainland, and demonstrating how the design is to retain the island's wetlands landscape in its development.

transport. It also has to be remembered that Dongtan is at present a masterplan. In the long term, the whole-scale implementation of environmental measures will depend on the client and future investors overseeing the development and, ultimately, the citizens and local government. Arup can do no more than provide them with the tools and guidelines for sustainable development.

There is no doubt that at Dongtan Arup have incorporated a well-researched sensitivity to the Chinese urban context, incorporating a sense of place and culture in their planning. It remains to be seen how true to this sensibility the execution of Dongtan and other eco-cities will remain. Faced with the real prospect of dwindling resources and the pressing need to accommodate an ever-expanding urban population, the Chinese government may have more 'scientific' rather than social concerns, as highlighted by CJ Lim of Studio 8 who has developed designs for Guangming Smart City in China (see his Practice Profile, pp 110–17): 'The Chinese government has recently presented their new ecological showcase city to the United Nations World Urban Forum – the focus sadly was very much on energy and the environment only. Important social and economic questions were ignored. Can rapid economic growth be cultivated in a rural setting and stop the migration of its skilled inhabitants? How can economic growth in a rural environment be encouraged while preserving tradition and maintaining social sustainability?'[12] The success of the city as both a socially as well as an environmentally sustainable scheme rests on the client. As Peter Head has suggested, all the indications are good. SIIC have taken a keen interest in the UK definition of mixed-use development, incorporating housing for those on lower incomes and key workers as well as wealthier occupants. For this important, flagship eco-city, though, the proof will ultimately be in the making. ⚿

Notes

1. Richard Register, *Ecocity Berkeley: Building Cities for a Healthy Future*, North Atlantic Books (Berkeley, CA), 1987. In an email of 9 May 2008, Richard Register pointed out to me that the term 'eco-city' was in fact formulated previously 'in the winter of 1979–80 sometime when we were reorganising an organisation of which I was the founding President, Arcology Circle, Inc, which was interested in Paolo Soleri's ideas of three-dimensional cities in single structures or effectively single-structure with buildings being linked on many levels above ground level.'
2. See Herbert Girardet's new chapter on eco-cities including Dongtan in *Cities People Planet: Urban Development and Climate Change*, 2nd edn, John Wiley & Sons (Chichester), April 2008.
3. Herbert Girardet quoted from an email to Helen Castle, April 2008.
4. 'China overtakes US as world's biggest CO_2 emitter', *Guardian*, 19 June 2007. See http://www.guardian.co.uk/environment/2007/jun/19/china.usnews
5. 'An Overview of Urbanization, Internal Migration, Population Distribution and Development in the World', United Nations Population Division, UN/POP/EGM-URB/2008/01, 14 January 2008. See http://www.un.org/esa/population/meetings/EGM_PopDist/P01_UNPopDiv.pdf
6. Interview with Peter Head at Arup in London, February 2008.
7. Douglas McGray, 'Pop-Up Cities: China Builds a Bright Green Metropolis', *Wired* magazine, issue 15.05, http://www.wired.com/wired/archive/15.05/feat_popup.html
8. Details of the MoU agreement are from Arup's MoU Final Press Release of January 2008. See also 'Brown sees "green" sites in China', 19 January 2008: http://news.bbc.co.uk/2/hi/uk_news/politics/7197501.stm
9. Email correspondence with Beth Hurran of Arup, 28 May 2008.
10. Steve Schiffores (Globalisation reporter, BBC News), 'China's eco-city faces growth challenge', 5 July 2007: http://news.bbc.co.uk/2/hi/business/6756289.stm
11. See Foster + Partners' project description of the Masdar development: http://www.fosterandpartners.com/Projects/1515/Default.aspx
12. CJ Lim quoted from email to Helen Castle, April 2008.

After China: The World?

Three Perspectives on a Critical Question

Are China's cities now poised for global influence? This challenging question initiates a tripartite response from three authors: **Kyong Park**, **Laurence Liauw** and **Doreen Heng Liu**. In order to fully speculate on the potential of Chinese urbanism and architecture beyond its own borders: Park looks at whether China is a fully replicable capitalist model; Liauw outlines recent indicators of urban Sinofication around the world, whether it is the exporting of high-end designer furniture to the West or the injection of Chinese capital into Africa; and Heng Liu examines the dissemination of the Pearl River Delta both as an idea — first proliferated by Rem Koolhaas in the mid-1990s — and in its physical manifestations.

Installation at 'China Design Now' exhibition at the
V&A, London, 15 March–13 July 2008.
This major international exhibition, featuring the three
main coastal cities of Shenzhen, Shanghai and Beijing,
effectively introduced a London audience to the
current creative energy of China.

The End of Capitalist Utopia?

By Kyong Park

With China's economic miracle continuing at a brisk rate, the idea of China eclipsing the West, through the globalisation of its capital and labour, is now turning into the question of whether the West, and the rest of the world, will gradually become China. Shadowing China's reputation as the 'factory of the world' is the immediate expectation that China will improve its educational, technological and cultural sectors, shifting it to a higher position in the globalised 'urban food chain' of design, and technology- and construction-related services. China could be poised to bring forth its own brands and systems at the higher ends of the global economy.

Is China is regaining its status as the centre of the world – as its name itself implies? (*Zhong Guo*, the Chinese word for China, literally means 'Middle Kingdom', placing the country at the centre of the world and foreign territories at the periphery.) In the midst of its modernisation process, it is literally manufacturing cities from scratch; with more than 166 cities populated by over one million inhabitants already (the US has only nine such cities), and 400 new cities in the pipeline over the next 20 years, China is already consuming 'half of the world's cement, a third of its steel and over a quarter of its aluminum'.[1]

However, this also means that China's absorption of natural resources and energies may grow and surpass those that were previously expended by the rest of the world. The global problem is that the arrival of China as a major consumer of natural resources is occurring as we approach – if we have not already passed – the peak of energy production from fossil fuels.[2] It then is clear that the future of China rests on the natural resources needed to fuel its current ascendancy, as this is inextricably tied to a vicious cycle of material production and consumption that is most acute in cities. The question should be asked whether China is producing new urban paradigms that could meet the historical challenges of the energy equation. (For further details on China's ecodesign initiative, see Helen Castle's article in this issue: 'Dongtan, China's Flagship Eco-City: An Interview with Peter Head of Arup', pp 64–9.)

Rather than be intoxicated by the speed and scale of its urban development, China may have yet to invent a new urban paradigm beyond localised adaptations of

The current rise of China may not be so different from the path of developed nations. China's urban development paradigms may best be learned from Detroit, a shrinking city, rather than Dubai, an expanding city in China's mould.

global industrialisation, modernisation and urbanisation models, which still remain the dominant protocols for the capitalisation of a society. The current rise of China may not be so different from the path of developed nations. China's urban development paradigms may best be learned from Detroit, a shrinking city, rather than Dubai, an expanding city in China's mould. The cities in the Pearl River Delta (PRD), China's factory belt, for instance, share ultimately more in common with Detroit, one of America's most important manufacturing bases in the 20th century and the nation's centre of car production, than Dubai, which has shifted in recent years from an economy based on oil to that of financial services, property and tourism.

The economic utopia of perpetual growth is facing unsustainable reality in China. Just as the shortage of consumer products was partially responsible for the demise of communism in the USSR, neo-liberalist capitalism may ironically unravel the planned capitalist economy of China, most evidently under strain in its army of emerging cities. Certainly, for the 'factory of the world' the next few years should prove telling if consumer markets in the West continue to retract, and the efficiency of the planned economy and political centralism continues to be tested by recession and environmental challenges – whether natural disasters or diminishing resources.

Notes
1. 'The new colonialists', *The Economist*, 13 March 2008.
2. In 1956, geologist Dr M King Hubbert predicted that the production of oil from conventional sources would peak in the US between 1965 and 1970 (the actual peak was in 1970) and that a worldwide peak would occur around now. For more on his predictions, see M King Hubbert, 'Energy from Fossil Fuels', *Science Magazine*, Vol 109, No 2823, American Association for the Advancement of Science, 4 February 1949.

Huangpu District, Shanghai.
Large-scale construction projects in China, as elsewhere, often require the destruction of existing communities and the historic urban fabric. Here, a neighbourhood in the old city of the Huangpu District of Shanghai has been demolished.

Interchange #3 of Sheikh Zayed Road, Dubai.
Parallels are often made between Dubai and China's cities in terms of the velocity and scale of construction. Here, in Dubai, half-finished structures and empty property await development.

The northwest section of Detroit.
Could China's manufacturing cities ultimately share the same destiny as Detroit? Once a boom town, its status as the automobile manufacturing capital of the world has diminished. The dilapidation of the urban fabric is apparent in this photo of a community decimated by the construction of a highway.

Exporting China

By Laurence Liauw

Global outsourcing flows of architectural and construction services. As shown here, China is at the centre of a huge global network as the international centre for architectural and construction outsourcing.

The exporting of Chinese architecture and urbanism, in terms of practice, building types and culture, suggests the possibility of a recent urban 'Sinofication of the World'.[1] This view of China as a proactive creative and commercial force is one that is currently being put forward by architectural observers and critics to counterpoint the received notion of China as a 'globalised' nation.[2] It balances out the emphasis that has been put on the massive influx of Western capital and architectural design into China by also underlining the extensive output of Chinese architectural and construction services and products; it also recognises the wider side effects of urbanisation, such as consumption, inflation and tourism. The question remains whether this output constitutes an emerging urban culture and practice that may be regarded as influential globally, independent of China's own growth. Conversely, should it be viewed simply as the manifestation of excess capacity and economic expansion in architectural and urban production?

Products and Prefabricated Construction

Numerous Chinese-manufactured building components are penetrating world markets, especially in the prefabricated building construction sector. For example, in Hong Kong nearly all new public housing now uses Chinese-prefabricated concrete panels for its construction and Chinese-fabricated integrated glass units for curtain-walling. Italian company Permastalisa, one of the world's premier cladding design-fabricators, has curtain-wall and aluminium cladding manufacturing facilities in Dongguan in China that export to quality design projects around the world. Luxury five-star hotel furniture is now also being exported globally, produced by foreign-owned manufacturers often to internationally copyrighted designs.

State-owned China Construction and Infrastructure

The China State Construction Engineering Corporation (CSCEC) is China's largest state-owned construction conglomerate; it was ranked the world's 16th largest building contractor in 2002, with a total contract value of RMB502.6 billion with 28 per cent of its revenue coming from overseas contracts.[3] The corporation has many

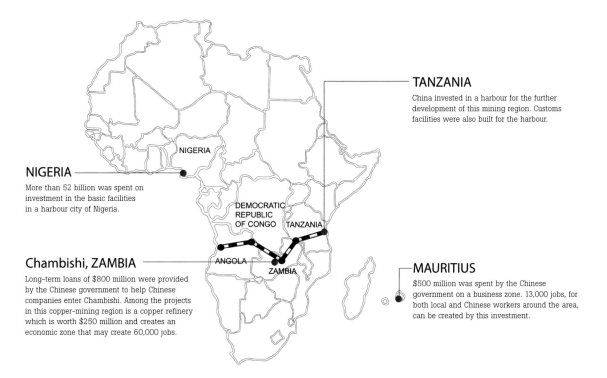

TANZANIA

China invested in a harbour for the further development of this mining region. Customs facilities were also built for the harbour.

NIGERIA

More than 52 billion was spent on investment in the basic facilities in a harbour city of Nigeria.

Chambishi, ZAMBIA

Long-term loans of $800 million were provided by the Chinese government to help Chinese companies enter Chambishi. Among the projects in this copper-mining region is a copper refinery which is worth $250 million and creates an economic zone that may create 60,000 jobs.

MAURITIUS

$500 million was spent by the Chinese government on a business zone. 13,000 jobs, for both local and Chinese workers around the area, can be created by this investment.

China has set up four African Special Economic Zones (SEZs). At the high-profile 2007 Beijing Forum on China–Africa Cooperation (FOAC), following the 2006 China–Africa summit attended by 48 heads of state, China stated its commitment to set up further zones in the region.

sub-branches that have been internationally active in building projects over the past two decades. This is especially the case in Asia and developing countries, where the CSCEC has built projects such as bridges, railway lines, airports, power stations, malls (most notably the Burj Dubai development) and even artificial islands (such as the Palms Jimerah project in the United Arab Emirates).

The SEZ Model in Africa and Asia
In recent years capital, such as that of the state-owned China Investment Corporation with over US$200 billion in assets, has been pouring out of China to other countries.[4] If Chinese capital is the new export, then the accompanying development models are significantly visible in several African countries: Zambia, Mauritius, Tanzania and Nigeria have all set up Special Economic Zones (SEZs) financed by China in order to establish natural resource mining, manufacturing, ports and trade. China's trade with African countries increased to US$56 billion in 2006 with a target of $100 billion by 2010.[5] African countries have adopted China's SEZ model in both its financial and physical form (Special Economic Zones being particularly important in the genesis of China's recent economic reforms since the late 1970s). More than 900 company projects have been built, including farms, refineries, offices, plantations, schools, hospitals, stadia, railroads and power stations.[6]

In Vietnam, manufacturing facilities have shifted from China to new SEZ production hubs that are part of a changing Vietnamese market-oriented economy; a 700-hectare (1,730-acre) Nam Giang Border Economic Zone has, for instance, been established on Vietnam's border with Laos and Thailand.[7] This SEZ is a government-regulated area where investors operate the capitalist economy inside a socialist country. Other developing countries are also interested, indicating the global influence of this successful Chinese model. More SEZs will be set up in countries such as India, where a 2005 SEZ Act was passed; in Cambodia, where a 11-square-kilometre (4.2-square-mile) Sihanoukville Special Economic Zone is being undertaken as a joint venture with China;[8] in Indonesia, where 10 new SEZs are being proposed; and in Ukraine and Russia, where six new SEZs are under way.[9]

Digital Rendering and Model-Making
Due to the construction boom and competitive standards of architectural competition presentations in China, a new industry of digital rendering and model-making was spawned in the 1990s. Expert companies began to dominate the world market using the latest in digital rendering, modelling and animation techniques. Market leader Crystal CG (Crystal Digital Technology Co Ltd) has offices in Singapore and Hong Kong as well as six in mainland China.[10] They serve clients undertaking projects in China, such as the Beijing Olympics and CCTV, as well as elsewhere in the world, and they have a US website that caters specifically for a US client base. Similarly, Chinese architectural model-makers use the latest

techniques in digital fabrication to make physical models in China and export these overseas for projects conceived by both Chinese and international practices.

Architecture Students and Academics

Chinese architects have been studying abroad since the early 20th century, but it was not until the 1990s, when a new generation educated in the West returned home and spread their wings globally, that the tables were turned. After finishing his education at Berkeley and having taught in the US for 15 years, architect Yung Ho Chang was among the first to establish an independent practice in China, setting up Atelier FCJZ with his partner Lija Lu in 1993. The founding Head of the Graduate Center of Architecture at Peking University, in 2005 Chang was appointed Professor of Architecture and Head of the Department of Architecture at MIT in Boston, which provided international recognition of China's academic influence. Subsequently architect Ma Qingyun, founding principal of Shanghai firm MADA s.p.a.m. (see pp 84–5), was appointed Dean of the USC School of Architecture and holder of the Della and Harry MacDonald Dean's Chair in Architecture in January 2007. Increasingly, Chinese architecture and urban scholars are 'exported' around the world's important architectural educational institutions, with many remaining active in practice. In the 2008 UIA Congress student design competition, eight out of nine top student design prizes were awarded to participants from China.[11]

The International Rise of the Chinese Architect

The practising architects returning to China from abroad over the past 10 years have been rewarded with ample opportunities to experiment and build what is not often easily possible overseas, spawning a culture of progressive architecture. In the past two years notable young Chinese architects are beginning to build significant

In the planned Saadiyat Island Cultural District in Abu Dhabi, UAE, which is currently under construction, Chinese architect Zhu Pei has been commissioned by the Guggenheim Foundation to build an art pavilion alongside museums by Frank Gehry, Zaha Hadid and Jean Nouvel.

MAD's design for a low-energy, lightweight prefabricated house-pavilion to be made in China and shipped to Denmark for assembly.

projects globally. Ma Yansong, founder of Beijing architectural firm MAD (see pp 92–3), is building two twisting residential towers in Canada and a prefabricated low-energy house-pavilion in Denmark. Zhu Pei of Beijing-based Studio Zhu Pei has been commissioned by the Guggenheim Foundation to design an art pavilion for the Saadiyat Island Cultural District in Abu Dhabi, and is being retained to design a potential museum for the Guggenheim in Beijing.[12]

Conclusion

China's urbanisation has triggered massive opportunities for those in the architecture, engineering and construction industries, and the diverse skills and experience in these sectors has begun to be exported globally. Whether this recent phenomenon represents a potential 'Sinofication of the World' or is merely a side effect of China's globalisation remains to be seen. However, what is emerging is an indication that Chinese design is on the rise globally, whether as an important cultural player or as a significant construction and production resource for architects and contractors worldwide.

Notes
1. See Ole Bouman (ed), in *Volume 8: Ubiquitous China, Archis*, No 2, 2006, pp 6–7, 18–19; Rem Koolhaas, in ibid, pp 120–26; Shumon Basar (ed), *Cities from Zero*, AA Publications, 2006; and Lauren Parker and Zhang Hongxing (eds), *China Design Now*, V&A Publishing, 2008.
2. The 'Exporting China' Symposium was organised by China Lab at Columbia University GSAPP on 16 February 2008. The contents of this article do not make any direct reference to the forum contents, although both titles are the same and some themes investigated may overlap. See also D Farrell, J Devan and J Woetzel, 'Where Big is Best', *Newsweek*, 26 May–2 June 2008, pp 45–6.
3. Statistics from the corporate website of the China State Construction Engineering Corporation (CSCEC): http://www.cscec.com.cn/english/co.htm.
4. Caijing Annual Edition, *China 2008 Forecasts and Strategies, Caijing* magazine, pp 18–20, 115 –16, 120–21, 124–25, 164–67.
5. Ibid.
6. Martyn Davies, 'China's Developmental Model Comes to Africa', *African Review of African Political Economy*, Vol 35, No 115, 2008. See also http://www.timesonline.co.uk/tol/news/world/africa/article3319909.ece.
7. http://en.wikipedia.org/wiki/Special_Economic_Zone.
8. Ibid.
9. Ibid. See also http://english.peopledaily.com.cn/english/200011/11/eng20001111_54882.html.
10. http://www.crystalcg.com/index.aspx.
11. http://www.totem.uia2008torino.org/vincitori.aspx.
12. http://archrecord.construction.com/features/designvanguard/07dv/07StudioPei-Zhu/07StudioPei-Zhu.asp

After the Pearl River Delta:[1]
Exporting the PRD – A View from the Ground

By Doreen Heng Liu

Rem Koolhaas' 2001 book *Great Leap Forward*, based on fieldwork undertaken with the Harvard Graduate School of Design in the Pearl River Delta (PRD) in 1996, has proved seminal. It has defined the way in which China's rapid transformation and ensuing urban chaos has been disseminated to the world. Most significantly, in this book Koolhaas advocated 'a new form of urban co-existence'.[2] On identifying this wholly new phenomenon, Koolhaas also invented 'a number of copyrighted terms' to analyse it and describe it to the world.[3] What exactly could this new form be that he alluded to in his reference to the hundreds of years of Western urbanisation or China's 'one hundred years without change'? When these very different urban conditions from very different moments of history suddenly conjoined and simultaneously confronted the West, the impact was one of 'the suddenness of a comet'.[4] China's long absence from the world stage made the impact of this exported knowledge of the PRD's urban chaos and its rapid flux all the greater on the West, given the general 'cloud of unknowing'.[5]

Instant Urbanisation

Driven by Deng Xiaoping's famous phrases 'to get rich is glorious' and 'no matter it is a white cat or a black cat, as long as it catches a mouse, it is a good cat',[6] the high speed and urgency of 'creating a completely new urban substance'[7] in the PRD in the late 1970s was a direct result of the massive and immediate demand of manufacturing production in the region; the area benefited from its location immediately adjacent to Hong Kong, which had already become a global city under British rule. Overnight, the region boomed, and a sea of migrant workers from elsewhere in China flooded into the factories at the peripheries of the towns and city centres. The labour-intensive manufacturing industries were, in the first instance, mainly labelled 'Made by Hong Kong'. At least 7 million labourers were employed by Hong Kong, which shifted its own manufacturing base to mainland China. By the beginning of the 1980s, the 'Made in Hong Kong' labels of the 1960s and 1970s had finally become 'Made in China – by Hong Kong'.[8] The popularity of the PRD as a production centre for the rest of the world was borne out by the competitive prices it offered, which were themselves a direct result of cheap labour and readily available natural resources. Simply evoked by the 'Made in China' label, the PRD had become the largest manufacturing export power in China and a major global centre.

'Made in China' has become a dominant economic phenomenon in the world, as Sara Bongiorni demonstrates in her acclaimed book *A Year without 'Made in China'*.[9] It has an entirely unprecedented impact on people's daily lives on the other side of the world. Bongiorni's US-based family spent a year attempting to avoid anything with a 'Made in China' label. However, the experience proved more difficult than anyone might have imagined. 'Made in China', she concludes, is as unavoidable to us today as 'Made in Taiwan' and 'Made in Hong Kong' were to us in the 1970s, and 'Made in Japan' and 'Made in Korea' earlier in the 20th century.

八十年代末罗湖区鸟瞰

Shenzhen generic city, Pearl River Delta, early 1980s.

The urbanism that has accompanied the 'Made in China' phase in the PRD can perhaps be best understood as a new form of urban condition, with its mushrooming highway-infrastructure and 'generic city' (a term copyrighted by Koolhaas).[10] As Koolhaas said, 'it is nothing but a reflection of present need and present ability. It is the city without history. It is big enough for everybody. It is easy, it does not need maintenance. If it gets too small it just expands. If it gets old it just self-destructs and renews. It is equally exciting – or unexciting everywhere. It can produce a new identity every Monday morning.'[11] The PRD became a super 'generic city' of 40 million inhabitants, created from randomness and organised chaos within just a few years.

However, as the old Chinese idiom says, 'thirty years river east, thirty years river west'. All fortunes come in cycles. Today the process of 'Made in China' is gradually winding down and undergoing a further economic transformation. As manufacturing shifts once again, 'Made in China' becomes 'made in another part of the world'. Increasingly expensive resources in the PRD have made the decline of manufacturing inevitable. The end of the era of labour-intensive production in the region has been further marked by the emergence of an increasing number of bourgeoisie, as China steps into another consumption cycle and a further phase in the economy.

Random and Controlled Urbanism

A side production of economic development in China has been years of unbridled urban sprawl, which has created 'a world without urbanism',[12] with only physical substance. Suddenly, however, the peripheral urban landscape has become dotted with endless theme cities – furniture city, lighting fixture city, fashion city, food city, massage city, 24-hour entertainment city. Previously these areas were individually composed of a series of autonomous showrooms with a homogenous theme; many smaller showrooms of the same kind collectively, intensively and instantly clustered until they eventually formed a 'city' of homogeneity. These 'cities' have become local, even international, business and tourist destinations, like the famous Dafen Oil Painting Village in Shenzhen, which was founded in 1989 by an oil-painting businessman from Hong Kong and has become the premier base of oil-painting production – originals and reproductions alike. Paintings are exported all around the world to North America, Europe, Australia and Asia, and Dafen's renown has become such that it draws in tourists from home and abroad.

Furthermore, such a popular, random urban form in the region is paralleled with another kind of urban strategy: controlled development managed by local governments.

Instant urbanisation: random theme cities in the PRD region.

Dafen Oil Painting Village in Shenzhen is one of the most famous theme 'cities' in the PRD and draws tourists from both home and abroad. Originals and reproductions are sold to wholesale distributors, galleries, hotels, restaurants and interior designers in China and throughout the world. With so many similar businesses in just one village, competition is fierce and prices aggressive.

It is claimed that the 'China Design Now' exhibition, which took place at the Victoria and Albert Museum, London, in spring 2008, was the largest festival of Chinese culture ever held in the UK.

This includes large-scale homogeneous theme projects also branded cities: university city, convention city, airport city, science city or eco-city. Such mono-types we may consider direct interpretations of economy of scale in physical form – a perfect economic model with 'Chinese characteristics'.[13] Could this urban mono-type branding of cities as homogeneous supersized products be considered 'new' city-making? This begs the question whether beyond China the generic Chinese city can be re-exported.

With Chinese Characteristics

While high-speed and large-scale urban development continues, energy consumption has forever been on the increase, eating into fast-depleting natural resources. This has seen sustainability surface as a critical agenda. In Prime Minister Wen's 2008 'Government Working Report' he predicted that this year would be 'the most difficult year' for China. Though this could apply to many aspects of the nation's current development, one of the concerns

that emerges in the report is how to balance large-scale but environmentally costly projects against the still high demand for rapid economic growth. It can be concluded from this that the physical 'production' of this phase of urbanisation – large and speedy – is only part of a greater process or cycle. An early or primary phase, it can be regarded as anxious but raw, hungry but dyspeptic.

So the Chinese perhaps have enough reasons to say that they are right to be fearless. It took Baron Haussmann only 22 years, from 1865 to 1887, to re-create Paris, transforming it into a metropolis of grand boulevards and the magnificent city centre that we know today. Once 'some importance' is attached to the physical environment, even if it is rough and ready, time may play a significant role in nurturing culture. If it stops growing, we can simply explode it and rebuild it afresh. Although the lifecycle is short and fast, it results in an ever-changing face of a city that could be vibrating and exciting. We are optimistic about the way we are creating Chinese cities today. Such is the hunger for change that it is possible to turn any negative into a positive. Such an ideology sounds familiar; it guided communist China for several decades. Sadly, however, in the mid-20th century it only resulted in poverty and isolation from the rest of the world. However, times have changed. Since China is already growing big and globalised, this fearless 'ideology' can be regarded as a unique Chinese characteristic, which can be exportable and marketable to the rest of the world.

Exporting China Now

Meanwhile, another dimension of urban (design) culture is developing in China with increasing global exposure in the past few years. Lauren Parker, who recently curated the 'China Design Now' exhibition at the Victoria & Albert Museum in London,[14] has predicted that if the rapid process of Chinese design culture 'carries on in the next three and four years, Chinese architects … will be seen as part of the international design community and not just singled out because they are Chinese'.[15] The 'Exporting China' Symposium at Columbia University,[16] initiated by China Lab, intentionally marked the beginning of the end – the end of massive architectural and urban production in terms of scale and speed; and the beginning of China's new emerging cultural and intellectual influence on the world. But exporting China or even exporting the PRD in the sense of urban culture needs critical mass in breadth and depth in order to have a profound influence on global design culture. China's urbanisation in terms of its 'scale and speed' is still singled out as particular to the Chinese context. Maybe only a fully cultivated Pearl River Delta model can be established as an influential Chinese model for the rest of the world. Architecture can only be influential once an overall collective design culture has formed critical mass.

So far, we are still somewhere between chaos and celebration, and no further. ⌂

'Exporting China' Symposium, Columbia University, New York, 16 February 2008. Conversation with speakers Mark Wigley, Yung Ho Chang, Ma Qingyun, Doreen Heng Liu and Ackbar Abbas.

China's urbanisation in terms of its 'scale and speed' is still singled out as particular to the Chinese context. Maybe only a fully cultivated Pearl River Delta model can be established as an influential Chinese model for the rest of the world.

Notes

1. The administrative sphere of the PRD is composed of the Pearl River Delta Economic Zone, which was designated by the Guangdong provincial government in October 1994 (Guangdong Provincial Planning Committee and Office for the Planning of the Pearl River Delta Economic Region 1996). The PRD includes two vice-provincial-level cities (Guangzhou and Shenzhen), seven prefecture-level cities (Zhuhai, Foshan, Jiangmen, Zhongshan, Dongguan, Huizhou and Zhaoqing), nine county-level cities (Zengcheng, Conghua, Huiyang, Taishan, Kaiping, Enping, Heshan, Gaoyao and Sihui), two counties (Huidong and Boluo), and a number of city districts under the jurisdiction of the cities at prefecture level and above.

2. Rem Koolhaas, 'Introduction', in Chuihua Judy Chung, Jeffrey Inaba, Rem Koolhaas and Sze Tsung Leong (eds), *Great Leap Forward: Harvard Design School Project on the City*, Taschen GmbH, 2001, p 28. Koolhaas created the term 'City of Exacerbated Differences', or COED, based on this emerging new urban condition.

3. Ibid, p 28. 'Copyrighted' in Koolhaas' reference represents the beginning of a conceptual framework to describe and interpret the contemporary urban condition in the PRD.

4. Ibid, p 28.

5. Ibid, p 28.

6. Deng Xiaoping was a prominent Chinese politician and reformer and the late leader of the Communist Party of China (CCP). Deng never held office as the head of state or head of government, but served as the de facto leader of the People's Republic of China from 1978 to the early 1990s. He pioneered 'Socialism with Chinese Characteristics' and Chinese economic reform, also known as the 'socialist market economy', and opened China to the global market.

7. Koolhaas op cit, p 27.

8. Tak Chi Lee and Ezio Manzini, 'Made "in/by/as in" Hong Kong', in *HK Lab*, Map Book Publishers (Hong Kong), 2002, pp 138–43.

9. Sara Bongiorni , *A Year Without 'Made in China': One Family's True Life Adventure in the Global Economy*, John Wiley & Sons Ltd (Chichester), 2007.

10. Rem Koolhaas and Bruce Mau, *S, M, L & XL*, Monacelli Press, 1995.

11. Ibid, p 1,250.

12. Rem Koolhaas, 'What Ever Happened to Urbanism?', in C Jencks and K Kropf, *Theories and Manifestoes of Contemporary Architecture*, Academy Editions (London and Lanham, MD), 1997, p 967.

13. The term refers to 'Socialism with Chinese Characteristics', an official term for the economy of the People's Republic of China in which the state owns a large fraction of the Chinese economy, while at the same time all entities participate within a market economy. This is a form of a socialist market economy and differs from market socialism and a mixed economy in that while the state retains ownership of large enterprises, it does not necessarily use this ownership to control or influence local interventions. See http://en.wikipedia.org/wiki.

14. 'China Design Now' was at London's Victoria & Albert Museum between 15 March and 13 July 2008.

15. Jessica Au, 'Not Just Made in China', *Newsweek*, 24 March 2008.

16. 'Exporting China' Symposium, 16 February 2008, organised by Mark Wigley and Jeffrey Johnson, China Lab, Graduate School of Architecture, Planning, and Preservation, Columbia University, New York. The symposium invited four guests – Yung Ho Chang, Ma Qingyun, Ackbar Abbas and Doreen Heng Liu 'to discuss the potential reciprocating influence of contemporary Chinese architecture & urbanism on global spatial practices worldwide' (quoted from the flyer for 'Exporting China').

Emerging Chinese Architectural Practice *Under Development*

China presents unique opportunities to design and build innovative architectural structures. **Laurence Liauw** showcases five nascent practices, still under development, **MADA s.p.a.m., URBANUS, Atelier Zhanglei, standardarchitecture** and **MAD** – who after having gained educations at top institutions in the US and Europe have come home to build cutting-edge designs that harness new technologies, creative processes and critical thinking.

MADA s.p.a.m. (Ma Qingyun)

Ma Qingyun graduated from Tsinghua University School of Architecture and the University of Pennsylvania (U Penn) before going on to gain extensive work experience at Kohn Pedersen Fox and Kling Lindquist in the US, and to lecture at U Penn and Shenzhen University. In 1999 he founded MADA s.p.a.m. (strategy, planning, architecture, media) in Shanghai as a result of his frustration with big corporate practice.

Driven by the 'blind faith' opportunities for building in China in the mid-1990s, in 1996 Ma returned to Shenzhen to collaborate with Rem Koolhaas on the landmark 'Great Leap Forward' Harvard Pearl River Delta (PRD) research project. At about the same time, his 'moonlighting' efforts while still teaching to nurture project opportunities focused on exploiting the skills gap between small atelier-style practices and larger corporate design institutes. His ability to operate with a small design team on big projects eventually led to his breakthrough competition-winning proposal for the massive Ningbo University masterplan, which would result in his first built project, the 4 million square-metre (43,055642 square-foot) Zhejiang University Library, completed in 2002.

Overnight, MADA s.p.a.m. increased in size from three to 30 staff, and now has more than a hundred employees, allowing 'excess capacity' for speculative and research projects in addition to commercial ones. With offices in Shanghai, Xian, Beijing, Shenzhen and Los Angeles, such research is at the core of the practice's philosophy of engaging, with political intentions, in an open process with clients and intellectuals. MADA s.p.a.m. sees architecture not as just a finished product, but as a rigorous process that challenges dead-end ideas and strives for coherence. Ideas and practice are delayed, diverted and even destroyed in the constant questioning of each project beyond traditional building values. A relatively young practice (of less than 10 years), MADA is still 'under development' (with a high staff turnover and multi-timezone design management) armed with a self-organising, energetic and seemingly chaotic ethos of self-critique, coupled with Ma's 'hands-off practice' which allows him the distance from which to manage, protect and transform critical ideas through architecture and building.

After a string of high-profile projects including the masterplanning of new buildings, museum renovations and international biennales, in 2007 Ma Qingyun assumed the position of Dean of the School of Architecture at the University of Southern California, becoming only the second Chinese dean (after Yung Ho Chang of MIT) to lead a major US architecture school. This significant move back to academia while continuing to practise stretched his reach beyond China, enabling him to both import new ideas to China and export Chinese ones globally. He believes that 'new business' models hold the key to constructing new knowledge for future architecture: 'Practice is about proving truths and moral obligation, while business is about optimising the combination of differences, and can therefore be more innovative.' Surprisingly, he seems less anxious than the younger generation of up-and-coming progressive Chinese architects to demonstrate his ability 'to build well' in a traditional architectural sense. Bored with restrictive traditional methods of practice, innovation rather than performance is central to Ma's ambitions (beyond business and politics), and he has therefore established a new initiative, the CHI (Creative Humanitarian Initiative), with the aim of spreading creative initiative across China to benefit the wider society.

Zhejiang University Library, Zhejiang Province, 2002
The library is located on the Ningpo campus of Zhejiang University, which was also masterplanned by MADA s.p.a.m. It simultaneously occupies the hinge point between the living and teaching quarters, and its form follows that of an ancient Chinese scripture pavilion. The books, which are stable and permanent, are stacked along the building perimeter, enclosing readers, who are ephemeral and in constant flux, in a large void in the centre. In this traditional reading of space, the library makes a centre, but does not occupy it.

Ningbo Central Commercial District (Tian-Yi Plaza), Ningbo, 2002
Ningbo Central Commercial District, or Tian-Yi Plaza (Heaven One Plaza Hop), was perceived as a quick consolidation for the city's otherwise undefined urban identity. It is an extremely hypothetical project for MADA s.p.a.m., in which the following questions are constantly addressed: Does a city still need a centre? What is the role of construction in urbanism? What does shock or interruption mean for a city? Can megastructure be recomprehended for minuscule intervention? How does the traditional practice of architecture cope with the new mobility of urbanisation?

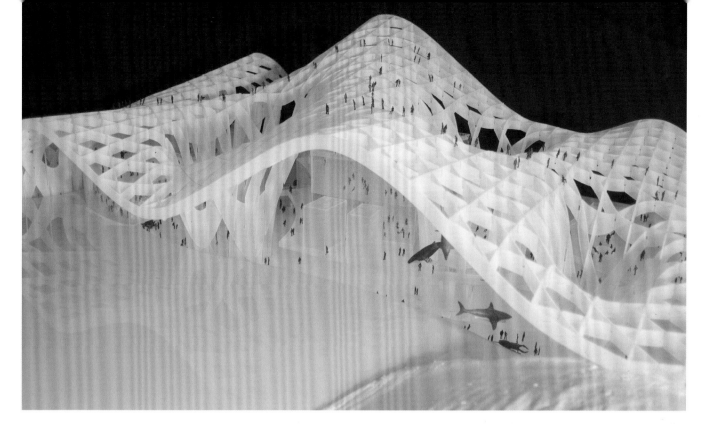

Xinyu Natural History Museum, Xinyu, Jiangxi Province, competition, 2007

The museum was conceived not only as an abstract 'natural expression' of architecture for enjoyment, but also to evoke people's imagination regarding the contemporary landscape, humanity, space and time. In the centre of a lake, the building also acts a bridge, and the flexible interior mixes museum space with leisure, entertainment and views of the surrounding landscape. Environmental awareness is emphasised via imagery of the museum contents, and also by the green technology incorporated within the building design.

MADA s.p.a.m. frequently engages in experimental competitions (most recently in Vietnam and France) and speculative projects, such as the re-forming of Hainan Island, through self-initiated international design workshops with local governments, aimed at creating new potentials for architecture. This sense of exploration also underpinned Ma's recent efforts as chief curator of the Shenzhen–Hong Kong Bi-City Biennale of Urbanism and Architecture (2007), where he developed the main theme of the exhibition through 10 critical curatorial questions about the expiry and regeneration of the 30-year-old Shenzhen city and commissioned 20 research projects on the 'Future of the City' relating to these questions.

Apart from the multitude of commercial and public architecture projects on hand, Ma has branched out into education, curatorship, museum management (the Xian Center of Modern Art) and conceptual art, and has built and now runs his own hotel and vineyards in Xian. He is also planning to set up a new breed of design school, one where design is multidisciplinary and is information-based, not based solely on the production of the physical. One wonders whether MADA s.p.a.m.'s future ambitions will lead to new things including and beyond buildings, and whether Ma's generation of reactionary experimental architects could eventually lead the charge (through practice and rhetoric) to foster a Chinese avant-garde in architecture.

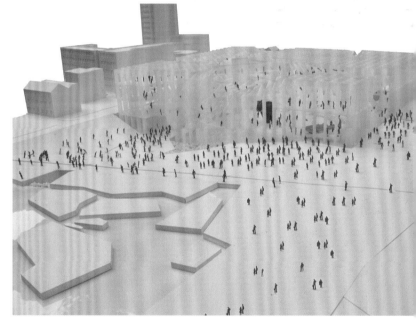

Shanghai Natural History Museum, Shanghai, competition, 2006

The museum is an attempt to demonstrate Shanghai's dedication to environmental concerns and public spirit in architecture through the concept of 'One Building, Two Places'. Below the huge roof that defines the building's form are the Natural History Museum exhibition spaces, while the roof top provides the foundations for the Nature Experiential Garden. The undulating form of the roof results in the varying heights of the internal spaces where the different exhibition scenes collide within the vast and continuous expanse of the museum. The outdoor Nature Experiential Garden and integrated sculpture park mix various regional cultures and reflect different seasons, encouraging a healthy interaction between urban life and nature.

URBANUS Architecture & Design (Liu Xiaodu, Meng Yan + Wang Hui)

Despite having gone to university several years apart, the founding partners of URBANUS – Liu Xiaodu, Meng Yan and Wang Hui – all took the same educational route. They are all graduates of Tsinghua University School of Architecture in northwest Beijing (where Liu Xiaodu also taught in the late 1980s) and undertook postgraduate studies at the University of Miami, in Oxford, Ohio. They also pursued work experience in large practices in the US: Meng and Wang in New York, at Kohn Pedersen Fox and Gensler respectively, and Liu in an office in Atlanta.

During the 1990s, URBANUS evolved through a long-distance, informal collaboration while Meng and Wang were still in New York and Liu was in China moonlighting on competitions. This Tsinghua/Miami University clique maintained sustained conversations about new architecture in China and shared the desire to collaborate in the future. As well as being devoted to architecture, they had ideals in common and a strong compulsion to take risks and do something different. They were the first generation of '*hai-gua*' (overseas-educated architects returning home) at a time when China's architecture was still developing. In 1997 Liu secured the chance to work on a government-commissioned urban-design proposal for Shenzhen's main boulevard pocket spaces, which led to the practice's first built project, Diwang Urban Park, in 1998 (completed in 2000). On New Year's Day 1999, URBANUS was founded.

The name URBANUS is derived from the Latin word for 'urban', and strongly reflects the practice's design approach: reading architectural programme from the viewpoint of the ever-changing urban environment. URBANUS is committed to the belief that architecture is a pivotal force for a better life and a progressive force in society. Moderating their way of working after returning to China, the partners maintained key ideas and theoretical influences – Shenzhen's chaos, where they first gained work, is quite different from that of other Chinese cities and is perhaps more compatible with Koolhaas' *Delirious New York* – very generic but full of potential to grow through self-organisation. This freedom at ground level is matched by the theoretical promise of Shenzhen being China's experimental 'window on the world': this one-time fishing village in Southern China, in close proximity to Hong Kong, was singled out in 1979 by the Chinese government to be China's first Special Economic Zone (SEZ), and since then has been one of the fastest-growing cities in the world. So urbanism has driven the practice, which always asks what architecture is needed for each site, what does the city need?

URBANUS' first two years of practice involved winning many competitions, and unbuilt proposals for urban parks and small projects, until they landed their first major commission to build the new headquarters for the Shenzhen Planning Bureau (SZPB). Their steady progress – they remained true to their core ideas – led to larger-scale projects, and URBANUS' reputation grew with the Shenzhen construction boom in 2001–03. URBANUS decided to focus on public buildings and keep the practice relatively small (starting with a staff of around 40, which has now grown to 70), subsequently winning competitions to build corporate headquarters, the SZPB and metro stations. With the Shenzhen office stabilised, Wang Hui moved to Beijing, the centre of China's architectural culture, in 2003 following the partners' original plan to set up there. The Beijing office was set up just as development of Northern China in preparation for the Olympics took off. Both offices operate separately, but share the same ideals, and design as a single practice according to location and conceptual platform. All three partners maintain constant critical involvement in each other's projects, and strive to experiment consistently without adopting a style or formal language – in that sense URBANUS is still 'under development', experimenting with each project's potential to reformulate the city.

Liu comments on the narrow repetitive styles of Chinese practices without criticism. The same narrow spectrum of progressive architects seems to be involved in most of the significant projects today, yet there is little discussion of the quality of the architecture being produced. URBANUS cares much about the professional standard of architecture in China, unlike practices that use irony and artistic temperament or ignore urban issues. Architecture cannot be just a personal thing, and URBANUS does not rely on tradition, although it cares about Chinese ideas and contemporary Chinese society. URBANUS could be on the edge of becoming the corporate mainstream with big commercial projects, but it is still retaining critical research that scrutinises its own work and allows the practice to be an experimental platform, through staff ideas and projects. But can URBANUS help to grow future generations of progressive architects after kick-starting this generation? Liu believes they may have only limited years of influence left, given the rate of change in China.

Diwang Urban Park, Shenzhen, Guangdong Province, 2000
Neighbouring the Diwang Tower (Shenzhen's tallest building), the design for URBANUS' first realised project weaves together a network of public spaces and the city's road system to provide a comfortable, green venue for various public activities.

Dafen Art Museum, Shenzhen, Guangdong Province, 2007
The museum is a unique project for both the city of Shenzhen and for the museum's architects. Located on the outskirts of the city, in Dafen Oil Painting Village, which is best known for producing forgeries of world-famous (and obscure) paintings, this mixed-use art centre responds to both the topography and unique cultural setting of its urban environment.

Vanke-Tulou Programme, Nanhai, Guangdong Province, due for completion 2008

This proposal for urban communal-living complexes for low-income residents is based on the centuries-old building tradition of the Hakka *tulou*, a unique form of architecture developed by the Hakka people of the mountainous Fujian Province, near Guangdong in Southern China. The Hakka *tulou* (literally, earth buildings) were usually square or circular enclosures with thick earth walls housing as many as 80 families. URBANUS' proposal integrates living spaces, entertainment, a small hotel and shopping within a single entity, and explores ways in which the city's green areas, roads and other spaces can be left relatively untouched by urbanisation by integrating new housing for the increasing population within the existing city fabric.

China Central Television (CCTV) Media Park, Beijing, competition, 2006

This open space within the CCTV Headquarters complex designed by OMA (now under construction) is a raised platform that takes its inspiration from Rem Koolhaas' pixel concept for the CCTV masterplan. A variety of shrubs and trees is used to represent the pixels, forming a forever-changing pattern to make this public space more enjoyable and engaging.

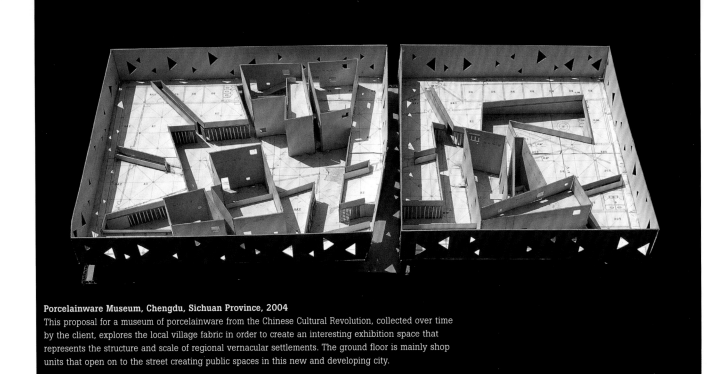

Porcelainware Museum, Chengdu, Sichuan Province, 2004
This proposal for a museum of porcelainware from the Chinese Cultural Revolution, collected over time
by the client, explores the local village fabric in order to create an interesting exhibition space that
represents the structure and scale of regional vernacular settlements. The ground floor is mainly shop
units that open on to the street creating public spaces in this new and developing city.

Atelier Zhanglei (Zhang Lei)

Zhang Lei studied architecture at the Nanjing Institute of
Technology and completed his postgraduate studies at ETH
Zurich. After 12 years teaching at China's Southeast University,
ETH Zurich and the Chinese University of Hong Kong, he founded
Atelier Zhanglei (AZL) in Nanjing in 2000. The same year he was
also appointed Director of the new Nanjing University
Architecture Design Institute (NJUDI) to oversee architectural
building projects on campus.

Currently dividing his time between mainly private practice
(AZL), administration (NJUDI) and teaching (he is now Vice-Dean
of Nanjing University), Zhang Lei combines theory and practice in
his building designs, which test his research at a 1:1 scale and at
the hyper-speed of China's growing built economy. The practice's
early designs include several buildings within university
environments, such as the NJU Graduate Student Dormitory, Staff
Residence at Dongguan Institute of Technology and the Model
Animal Genetic Research Center in Nanjing. All were executed in
short periods between 2000 and 2004, and quickly raised Zhang
Lei's international profile at a time when emerging Chinese
architects began attracting interest from the West.

Central to AZL's design philosophy is the investigation of
innovative building types and construction methods drawing from
local techniques and materials. The practice's belief that real
experience and the complexity of building sites can actually re-
inform architectural thinking and vice versa produces a tangible
cycle of integrated research, innovation and building. Such
integration is exemplified by AZL's recent Suzhou courtyard
houses design (2007), which applied contemporary interpretations
of Suzhou's classical gardens (elemental stone, water and bamboo)
by students from Japan's Chiba University to three urban
courtyard houses. A process of discovery, learning and application
underlines AZL's approach, and is proving to be a healthy model
for the upgrading of China's architectural industry, and for the
development of academia through experimental buildings.

In early 2001, international recognition of AZL's completed
campus buildings at NJU provided the opportunity for the
practice to join other emerging contemporary Chinese architects in an exhibition
at the renowned Aedes Gallery in Berlin. The Chinese media were quick to latch
on to this international exposure and, with the increasing appetite for the 'new'
in China, AZL was subsequently invited to collaborate on numerous
masterplanning and team building projects across the country, including the
high-profile Jianchuan Museum Cluster in Anren, Sichuan (2003), masterplanned
by Yung Ho Chang, one of China's most accomplished contemporary architects
and now Head of MIT's Department of Architecture. This phenomenon of
throwing together China's progressive 'starchitects' on the same site recalls the
fruitful international collaborations curated by Arata Isozaki in Japan in the
1980s, especially in Fukuoka, and has proved particularly successful for public
buildings such as museums and universities that require a unique identity and
differentiation from mass-produced design.

The above highlights a critical junction in China's global design arena after
2000, when the world began to take more serious notice of the country's
progressive architects (after Yung Ho Chang had solely led the way in the early
1990s), a development accompanied by a strengthening local identity among
those architects building experimental designs (without having to go through
the 'paper architect' phase of their Western counterparts).

For the future, AZL is seeking to address the social responsibility of mass-
market architecture within China's rapid urban development. Beyond small-scale
experimental architecture, Zhang Lei is looking forward to the challenge of
larger urban projects (such as building towers) that could affect the lives of
many, and transform local contexts and society in general. Basic design using
local construction techniques and exploring the tectonic innovations of
economical materials continue to underpin Zhang Lie's work in new types of
projects (his concrete Split House, a brick factory and the N-Park Jiangsu
software park). But the real challenge will come when, either through his AZL
practice or the NJU Design Institute, he starts to build at a much bigger urban
scale. The test for Zhang Lie will be whether the integrity of his sensitive design
process and innovative construction techniques can hold up to the harsh realities
of time, economy and skill in the new urban China.

Text © 2008 John Wiley & Sons Ltd. Images: pp 88, 89(t) © AZL Atelier Zhanglei; p
89(b) © Iwan Baan

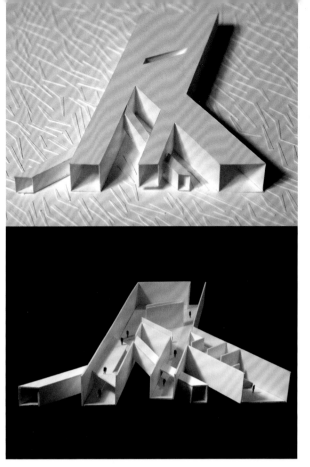

Nanjing Foreign Language School Student Dormitory, Nantong, Jiangsu Province, 1999
AZL's first built project reflects Zhang Lei's architectural language with a pure geometric logic of solids and voids. The low-budget project used basic materials such as brick and concrete, and exploited local traditional construction methods.

Fanglijun Art Gallery, Chengdu, Sichuan Province, due for completion 2008
Currently under construction, the Fanglijun Art Gallery will house works by one of China's most prominent contemporary artists. The building uses a repetitive Y-shape as its basic element to create a tree-like branching structure, and explores how a new exhibition space can gently fit into the beautiful forest landscape. Green glass fragments in the facade and the roof will be constructed using local masonry techniques.

Split House, Nanjing, Jiangsu Province, 2007
In keeping with the low-rise, high-density urban context of Nanjing, which was established in the 1920s, the Split House is a small, concrete project with a clear layout and minimal facade details. The wooden strip formwork on the concrete facade respects the scale and grain of the surrounding brick buildings, and the split between the two volumes of the house creates interesting interior spaces such as the stairwell and various family rooms.

standardarchitecture (Zhang Ke, Zhang Hong, Claudia Taborda + Hou Zhenghua)

Dancing Book Towers, Wuhan, Hubei Province, due for completion 2009

Of the two 150-metre (492.1-foot) high skyscrapers that make up this scheme, the first will be a single apartment per floor residential building with a typical floor plan of about 360 square metres (3,875 square feet), and the other will be a five rooms per floor hotel, with each floor measuring about 450 square metres (4,843.7 square feet). The 'dancing' of the shifting plans on alternate levels and the twisting perspective from the street create an ever-changing combination of gestures, transmitting an enchanting atmosphere to the urbanscape of Wuhan's Wu Chang City.

Zhang Ke graduated from Tsinghua University School of Architecture and then from the Harvard Graduate School of Design, after which he worked in New York. His practice, standardarchitecture (SA), was officially founded in 2001, in Beijing (evolving from his private practice in New York which he had established two years earlier) based on a long-distance collaboration with partner Zhang Hong, an experienced architect from Tsinghua's Architectural Design and Research Institute. Landscape architect Claudia Taborda, from Portugal, whom Zhang met at Harvard, and Hou Zhenghua complete the partnership.

While Zhang Hong is familiar with the processes of architectural practice in China, Zhang Ke pushes the culture for refined detailed design. It was their competition-winning proposal for the 2001 Beijing DongBianMen Ming Dynasty City Wall Relics Park that convinced Zhang Ke and Zhang Hong to establish SA, and participate in more (winning) competitions over the next two years, until their first projects were built in 2003 and 2005. The first, the Wuyi Elementary School Auditorium (designed in two weeks between New York and Beijing) was widely published, and the second building, the Yangshuo Storefronts retail and apartment complex in Guilin, Guangzi Province, won a World Architecture (China) Award.

In the Chinese language, the name standardarchitecture alludes to a neutral, anti-specific style of practice, focusing on fundamental ways of construction that are stripped bare of ornamentation and excess.

The turning point for the practice was the opportunity to oversee, as a client-appointed lead consultant, the design and construction of the Yangshuo Storefronts complex from start to finish, a process that at the time was rare among Chinese practices. The innovation, quality and expertise they demonstrated from conception to final execution of the project enabled them to raise their profile significantly and thus command higher fees for their comprehensive service.

The practice has since gained a solid reputation for its contemporary manner of working within traditional urban contexts, using local materials creatively, reinterpreting traditional methods of architecture, and inventing streamlined, minimal construction details in a non-institutionalised way. Another achievement came with the concrete realisation of an idealised scheme: Zhang Ke's Chinese inkbrush drawing for the Wuhan CRLand French-Chinese Arts Centre (2005). At its conception, the building was deemed structurally dangerous by local design-institute engineers due to the multiple 'random' voids cut into its structural walls. SA subsequently proposed incorporating a thick, hollow structural beam concept within the perforated building form and, having won over the structural

Wuyi Elementary School Auditorium, Beijing, 2003

This 500-seat, low-budget school auditorium, with its folded red-brick roof, creates an ironic allusion to the decades-old debate about the integration of traditional spatial concepts within modern Chinese architecture. It is used by both the school and local residents for stage performances, films and public gatherings. The rear wall and facade fold upwards as a continuous concrete surface to form the roof, which is also supported on both sides by a row of columns. Behind the columns, the enclosed galleries also have recessed red-brick walls. The entrance pierces the vertical wall of the front facade that folds upwards again to rise and cantilever from the ground as a continuous expression of the roof structure.

engineers and local design institute with this solution, the building, which was originally designed as a CRLand sales office, has been converted into an arts centre used for public events and exhibitions, and has become an iconic cultural city landmark.

SA's mission is not just about making beautiful buildings as collectibles, but also about raising questions about society and the city, and moving away from the insulated urban idealism that has typified the work of previous generations of China's architects. Their architecture involves the making of new object-types in the city to confront the existing urban context in a culturally sincere way, with new uses of local materials to maintain the continuity of the urban fabric, and a strong affinity to landscape design and urban materiality. Examples of this can be seen in a number of their projects currently under construction. In Tibet, SA is planning and building several new ecological resort cities along a 60-kilometre (37.3-mile) river canyon range, and in Wuhan an ambitious twin 50-storey Dancing Book Towers scheme will see stacked super-density towers and new courtyard houses joined by landscape design contributing to the urban fabric.

The future, according to Zhang Ke, lies in opening the practice up to new ideas by branching out into different areas of design beyond architecture: regional planning, landscape and industrial design, fashion and food (he runs two successful and fashionable restaurants in Beijing). But the main focus of the practice remains to realise more, and more diverse, projects. SA believes that, combined with other fields of creativity, architecture can achieve the new freedoms that society requires, and challenge the suppression of traditional architectural processes. What remains to be seen (one wonders what the limits will be) for standardarchitecture's non-standard approach is whether this new breadth and freedom will sustain the depth and craftsmanship that has distinguished the practice in these first few formative years.

Wuhan CRLand French-Chinese Arts Centre, Wuhan, Hubei Province, 2005
The building was conceived as an urban container, within which art objects, events, concepts and multiple activities can flourish. The original concept was an abstract Chinese inkbrush-drawing exercise, which was later translated into a concrete structure. The entire building has a perforated hollow beam structure, and is now used for cultural events in the city centre.

Hong Kong West Kowloon Agri-Cultural Landscape, Hong Kong, 2008
Bringing agriculture back into the urban centre of the contemporary metropolis, the exterior of this 550-metre (1,804.4-foot) high, mountain-shaped 'skyscraper' building, an artificial landmass, is covered in terraced paddy fields, while theatres, museums and shopping malls occupy the interior. On the site of the urban void of West Kowloon Cultural District, the proposed design was exhibited at the 1st Hong Kong-Shenzhen Biennale of Architecture and Urbanism (as part of the Urban Void Group).

MAD (Ma Yansong, Yosuke Hayano + Dang Qun)

Originally from Beijing, young architect Ma Yansong graduated from the Yale School of Architecture in 2002, after studying at the Central Academy of Fine Art (CAFA) in Beijing. After a brief period at Eisenman Architects in New York, he moved to London to work for Zaha Hadid, his former tutor at Yale. And it was at Hadid's office that he met the Japanese-born project designer Yosuke Hayano, who shared his vision of building a New Asia.

On returning to Beijing in 2004, Ma taught architecture at CAFA for a while, but it was his involvement in invited competitions and collaborations with contemporary artists during this period that loosened his attitude to architecture, something that is also clearly apparent in his risk-taking approach to architectural design. His strong belief that new young practices can promote change in a Chinese market of generally poor-quality architecture is reflected in the name of the practice he would set up in Beijing later that year: MAD (suggesting being angry at, and critical of, the current architectural scene in China).

While in London, Ma and Yosuke Hayano had won the Shanghai Modern Art Park competition, which was to provide further opportunities in Beijing. Thus by the end of 2004 Yosuke Hayano and Shanghai-born, New York-based Dang Qun (an experienced architect whom Ma had met on an Internet community forum for Chinese architects in New York) had joined Ma as partners, forming a global collaboration between the three partners in New York, London and Beijing.

Ma's Floating Island New York experimental project of 2002, while he was still at Yale, was published in the Chinese media at the same time as the 911 terrorist attacks, bringing invitations to competitions for various public buildings throughout China. (He later adapted the Floating Island concept for Beijing, in 2006, to challenge the ongoing development of the city's Central Business District.) Though all of his winning entries were published with powerful digital imagery, only the Finding Meiosis Fishtank, New York (2004) was ever built, and won an AIA award. Tired of winning but not building in China, MAD had its breakthrough finally in 2006 when the practice won the international open competition to build the Absolute Tower in Mississauga, Ontario, Canada (due for completion in 2009). So successful was this 50-storey high-rise condominium (units sold out immediately at its launch), which will be the tallest multistorey building in Ontario outside of Toronto, and whose curvy form will rotate 390 degrees from bottom to top, that a second was commissioned for the same site, completing the Absolute World development of five towers in total.

This landmark international competition win for such a young Chinese architect caused a media explosion for MAD, and resulted in many commissions for the practice from powerful clients in China wishing to express their ambition with something new and 'world class'.

Since then, other accolades have included the Architecture League of New York, Young Architects Award 2006. The practice also had a solo exhibition, 'MAD in China', at the 2006 Venice Architecture Biennale, and in January 2008 held another 'MAD in China' exhibition at the Danish Architecture Centre in Copenhagen. The same year the firm published *MAD Dinner*, a book that

Absolute Tower, Mississauga, Ontario, Canada, due for completion 2009
The design of MAD's high-rise residential condominium forsakes simplistic Modernism and instead expresses the greater complexity and diversity of modern society through multiple nonlinear geometric designs, while also catering for social needs. Dubbed the Marilyn Monroe Building by critics because of its sensuous, curving design, its overwhelming success resulted in Ma being commissioned to design a second tower (seen here on the left), completing the Absolute World development of five towers in total.

Hong Luo Club, Beijing, 2006
In this complex three-dimensional curving structure, the vagueness and uncertainty between the internal spaces, and their fluctuating functions are designed to maximise the building's relationship with its natural surroundings through openness and form. This new space provides a retreat for city dwellers, away from the ordered rule of the real world and the modern city – a place where rules and orders are relaxed and reflect more the 'soft' rules of nature.

Finding Meiosis Fishtank, New York, 2004

The prophase of this experiment involved tracking the trajectory of a fish that inhabits the dynamic spatial organisation of a transparent environment. Stereolithographic modelling and digital fabrication techniques were then employed to allow the fish to circulate in a dynamic fluid space, resulting in the innovative architectural form shown here. This first 'built' architectural project is a dwelling for fish, instead of humans, reflecting MAD's constant experiments with nature.

introduces diverse viewpoints about MAD and its architecture from the various characters in Ma's architectural world (clients, engineers, artists, curators and contractors), and which will be further discussed at 10 'MAD dinners' around the world that will be attended by the architectural community in each location.

Ma fondly remembers his sense of exploration growing up in Beijing's *hutongs* (narrow alleys lined with traditional courtyard residences), but looks forward to a future generation of Chinese talent – after the Olympic boom: 'The China scene needs more young people; it is growing too fast now without slow time, leaving many contemporary urban topics such as nature, construction and politics unclear.' MAD sees each new project as a way of exploring and questioning such critical issues, even where this entails an element of adventure and risk. Ma's aim is to open doors for a younger generation of architects to broaden the panorama and quality of China's architecture. This emerging practice's position may not yet be as clear as its distinctive, individual design style, but it remains an experimental hothouse of early-30s architects. Ma believes the past few years are just the beginning and the field is open.

With the opening of a Tokyo office in 2007, MAD is now a 40-strong practice spanning the globe with projects in Tokyo, Dubai, Denmark, Canada, Hong Kong and Malaysia. This is China's youngest practice, and the one with the furthest international reach, and is one of few firms pushing the engagement of the latest digital design technology within complex forms. Currently advancing the architectural scene with both innocence and confidence, MAD's landmark urban projects have paved the firm's way to discussions with city mayors concerning how to change society through quality architecture.

With no desire to become multinational, Ma's meteoric rise and media status could be compared to that of his former tutor Hadid's architectural potential after she graduated from the Architectural Association in London (which Alvin Boyarsky likened to a 'comet's trajectory' in an interview with Hadid in the 1980s). The real challenge will be to execute such visions not just in China, but abroad as well (Ma believes that exporting China's talents still has long way to go). MAD is trailblazing a new generation into the future. It is certainly a practice that is fluid, mobile and free, like Ma's Meiosis fish swimming in urban China's stormy waters. ⚙

Floating Island, Beijing, 2006

A further development from his Floating Island New York project of 2002, Ma's Beijing Floating Island suggests what China's densely populated cities may look like in the future, and demonstrates his belief in the need for a literal connection between diverse urban programmes in three dimensions on the ground and above, rather than segregation, and not simply chasing building heights. Digital studios, multimedia business centres, theatres, restaurants, libraries, exhibition venues, gyms, and even a man-made lake, are elevated above Beijing's Central Business District, where they are connected horizontally in the sky, the small building footprint having minimum impact on the existing ground.

Chronology

of Main Government Policies Affecting Urbanisation in China: 1970–2007

Compiled by Sun Shiwen

Late 1970s Reform of the rural economic system encouraging villagers to *'Leave the land without emigrating from the village; and work in factories without settling in cities'*. Rural labour remains in rural areas.

1978 China's leader Deng Xiaoping introduces the Open Door Policy to attract overseas investment, proclaiming that *'to get rich is glorious'*.

1980 State Council establishes five Special Economic Zones (SEZs), the coastal cities of Shenzhen, Zhuhai, Shantou and Xiamen, plus Hainan Island, opening up the market to trade, communication and investment with the outside world. These are later followed by many more.

New urban development policy aims to *'control the scale of large cities, modest development of medium-size cities and active development of small cities'*.

1984 State Council further promotes the commercialisation of pilot city-housing developments to boost the country's real-estate business.

12th Communist Party of China (CPC) Central Committee proposes focusing on cities instead of rural areas to accelerate economic reform.

State approval given for 14 coastal port cities (Dalian, Qinhuangdao, Tianjin, Yantai, Qingdao, Lianyungang, Nantong, Shanghai, Ningbo, Wenzhou, Fuzhou, Guangzhou, Zhanjiang and Beihai) to be opened to overseas investment.

The expansion and economic growth of such developing coastal cities leads to the appearance of a large number of new townships nearby.

State Council allows state-owned construction enterprises, transportation and railway sectors to employ farmers as contract workers, thus farmers with technical expertise can settle in cities.

1988 People's Republic of China (PRC) Constitution amended. State-owned land usage rights can now be transferred commercially in lease form to end users by the state via local governments.

1989 PRC City Planning Laws introduce urban planning guidelines for different-sized cities so that earlier urban development policies can be implemented.

1992 Economic growth and urbanisation in China begin to accelerate.

In his historic Southern China tour speech, Deng Xiaoping declares *'Development as an essential criterion'*, stating also that *'Development is the last word'*, and reinforcing the general government policy of *'building socialism with Chinese characteristics'*. The country thus experiences a second real-estate boom in cities in coastal areas such as Hainan and Beihai, Guangxi.

State Council opens the doors of all the capital cities of the inland provinces and autonomous regions, and also establishes 15 trade zones, 32 state-level economic and technological development zones, and 53 high-tech industrial development zones in large and medium-size cities.

Land-market reforms open up China's property market. New regulations allow both the sale and transfer of the land-use rights of state-owned land (similar to the land leasehold system in Hong Kong) to individuals and corporations by municipal governments (representing the state) through auction, tender or negotiation. The cost of land-use rights depends on land-use type, location, density and neighbourhood.

1994 National reform of the tax system. Fixed revenues from property-related taxes payable to local governments must now be shared with central government. Taxes affected include urban land-use tax, real-estate tax, urban real-estate tax, land-occupied tax and land value-added tax.

1997 State Council lifts the restriction on the rural population registering for permanent residence. Farmers who have worked and lived in small cities for years, and who have bought a property in a county-level city, can now apply for urban 'citizen' status.

1998 15th CPC Central Committee proposes to *'develop small towns as a strategy for the development of the rural economy and society'*.

A landmark State Council policy declares that housing in urban areas will no longer be provided and distributed by the state, but must be purchased by citizens instead of being assigned or subsidised by their state-owned employers.

Commercial bank loans are granted to citizens by the People's Bank of China (PBOC) for housing purchase, adding to the liquidity of the real-estate market and increasing home ownership.

1999 Permanent resident (*hukou*, or 'citizen') status is granted to those living in cities for more than six months, as local governments strive for better accountability of their registered residents and central government aims for higher official urban population figures.

2001 State Council proposes simpler administrative procedures for rural populations transferring to small towns from the villages, as well as speeding up the urbanisation process by reforming the household registration system (*hukou*) of small towns. Migrant rural populations can now obtain urban *hukou* (citizen) status through their workplace, through a relative already resident in the town or, in some cases, through property acquisition.

2002 National Ministry of Land and Resources issues *'Provisions for the Granting of State-owned Leaseholds by way of an Invitation of Bids, Auction or Listing on a Land Exchange'*, requiring that land used for real-estate development must be transferred through auction (with transfer procedures and legal liabilities for different land uses), instead of direct negotiation with local government.

16th CPC Central Committee proposes *'building a well-off society, taking a new road to industrialisation and persisting in the coordinated development of large, medium and small cities and small towns along the path to urbanisation with Chinese characteristics'*.

2003 Third Plenum of the 16th CPC Central Committee proposes a policy of *'scientific development'* within the context of a harmonious society that puts the *'people first'* – a comprehensive, coordinated, sustainable policy promoting overall economic development and striking a proper balance between urban and rural development.

PBOC grants loan subsidies to domestic individuals wishing to purchase a second home for their own use only.

State Council implements *'Sustained and Healthy Development of the Real Estate Market'* by further opening up the commercial housing market in major cities to domestic local buyers, and removing previous restrictions and price controls on foreign and local property investors.

State Development and Reform Commission announces the *'China Programme for Sustainable Development at the Beginning of the 21st Century'*.

2005 State Council puts in place various macro-economic control measures to stabilise inflating house prices. The PBOC introduces macro-controls to restrict lending availability by raising the lending rate ratios of banks and cancelling property loan subsidies for qualified buyers, for example for a second home, to curb speculation.

Fifth Plenum of the 16th CPC Central Committee proposes building *'new socialist villages'* in rural areas to reduce the growing inequalities between urban and rural development. Plans for improvements in the social infrastructure of such rural areas include public health, education and social security, and productivity subsidy incentives for farmers.

2006 In an attempt to create more affordable housing for China's domestic market, and to reduce growing foreign investment in oversized apartments, the Ministry of Construction requires that at least 70 per cent of all new housing built in any city must be smaller units of less than 90 square metres (968.7 square feet).

2007 Ministry of Construction unveils a landmark state property law that, for the first time, protects the property rights of individuals.

State Council reviews methods to provide more subsidised housing for low-income households in cities. **⚙**

Contributors

Huang Weiwen gained his BArch and Master of Urban Planning and Design from Tsinghua University in Beijing. He practised architectural design and urban planning for a few years after graduation, and currently works on the administration of urban design at Shenzhen Municipal Planning Bureau (where he is Deputy Director of the Urban and Architecture Design Department). He was also one of the organisers of the 2005 and 2007 Shenzhen Biennales of Urbanism and Architecture. His designs were exhibited in the V&A 'China Design Now' exhibition at the Victoria & Albert Museum, London (2008).

Jiang Jun is a designer, editor and critic whose work focuses on urban research and experimental study, exploring the interrelationship between design phenomenon and urban dynamic. He founded Underline Office in late 2003, and has been the Editor-in-Chief of *Urban China* magazine since the end of 2004, while also working on his book *Hi-China*. His work has been presented at exhibitions such as 'Get It Louder' (2005/2007), the Guangdong Triennale (2005), the Shenzhen Biennale(2005/2007), 'China Contemporary' in Rotterdam (2006) and 'Kassel Documenta' (2007), and he has been invited to lecture at universities including Sun Yat-Sen, Beijing, CUHK, Harvard, UCL, Tokyo and Seoul. Born in Hubei in 1974, he received his bachelor's degree from Tongji University in Shanghai, and his master's from Tsinghua University in Beijing. He currently teaches at the Guangzhou Academy of Fine Arts.

Kuang Xiaoming gained his Master of Urban Design/Planning at Tongji University, Shanghai, and is a national registered planner and urbanologist. He is currently the General Editor of *Urban China* magazine, and a director of Studio 2, Tongji Urban Planning and Design Institute, and the Shanghai Huadu Advertising & Media Company.

Laurence Liauw is an associate professor at the Department of Architecture, Chinese University of Hong Kong. After graduating from the Architectural Association (AA) in London, he practised as an architect in the UK, Malaysia and mainland China, and currently practises in Hong Kong. His main area of interest is Asian urbanism types and parametric design. He has transformed the spaces of various social institution buildings in Hong Kong. Published internationally in a wide range of media including *World Architecture*, *Domus*, *Bauwelt* and *FARMAX* (010 Publishers), in 1997 he co-produced with the BBC a television documentary on the rapid urbanisation of the Pearl River Delta. He has won several invited architectural competitions and awards, exhibits works internationally, including at the 2006 Venice Biennale and the 2007 Hong Kong–Shenzhen Bi-City Biennale.

Doreen Heng Liu received her BArch from the Huazhong University of Science & Technology, China, and an MArch from the University of California Berkeley. She is currently a Doctor of Design candidate at Harvard Graduate School of Design, where her research focuses on contemporary urbanism in the Pearl River Delta, and the specific impact of urbanisation on design and practice in the Pearl River Delta today. She established her practice NODE (Nansha Original Design) in 2004, and is also chief architectural consultant for the Fok Ying Tung Foundation for the Nansha City development. Completed and current design projects include the Nansha Science Museum, Nansha Hotel Health Center, PRD World Trade Center Building, Artist's Studio for the Nanjing International Housing Exhibition, and the Qing Cheng Villa in Chengdu. She has been published in *Architectural Record* and *Domus*, and has participated in exhibitions including the Shanghai Biennale (2002), Venice Biennale (2003), Guangzhou Triennale (2005) and the Shenzhen Architecture Biennale (2007).

Born in Taiwan, **Liu Yuyang** received his MArch from Harvard Graduate School of Design and his BArch from the University of California San Diego. He carried out research with Rem Koolhaas in the late 1990s to publish *Great Leap Forward*, a book on the emerging urban conditions of China's Pearl River Delta. Having completed his first major commission, the Shanghai Museum of Contemporary Art, he now heads his Shanghai-based practice Atelier Liu Yuyang Architects. He previously taught at the Chinese University of Hong Kong and was recently invited to serve as one of the head curators for the 2007 Shenzhen–Hong Kong Biennale of Urbanism and Architecture.

Educated at TU Delft University and having previously worked at OMA, **Neville Mars** is currently an initiator of projects that include architecture, urban design, documentaries, art installations, urban research and creative writing. He is the Director of Dynamic City Foundation (DCF) in Beijing. The first three years of DCF research have been published in *The Chinese Dream: A Society Under Construction* (010 Publishers, 2008). The book is available in its entirety online and will further expand on http://BURB.tv, the world's first open-source design platform dedicated to the understanding and enhancement of China's cities.

Under the leadership of three partners, **Meng Yan**, Liu Xiaodu and Wang Hui, URBANUS Architecture & Design is an architectural practice and think tank providing strategies for urbanism and architecture in the new millennium. The name derives from the Latin word for 'urban', and strongly reflects the practice's design approach: reading architectural programme from the viewpoint of the urban environment in general and ever-changing urban situations specifically.

Kyong Park is an associate professor of public culture at the University of California San Diego, and was the founding director of the Centrala Foundation for Future Cities in Rotterdam. He is a founding member of the Lost Highway Expedition, which took place in August 2006 across nine cities in the western Balkans. He is the Editor of *Urban Ecology: Detroit and Beyond* (Map Office, 2005), was a co-curator for the 'Shrinking Cities' exhibition at the KW Institute for

Contemporary Art in Berlin (2004), the founding director of the International Center for Urban Ecology in Detroit (from 1999 to 2001), a curator of the Kwangju Biennale in South Korea (1997), and the founder/director of the StoreFront for Art and Architecture in New York (1982–98).

Shi Jian is currently Planning Director of ISreading Culture in Beijing. He has spent many years researching and reviewing the field of urban and architectural culture, and his work on this subject has been widely published and exhibited. He is a consultant to *Urban China* magazine, and an editor for *Avant-Garde Today* and *Building Review*. He participated, with Wang Jun, in the first Shenzhen Biennale of Urbanism and Architecture in 2005, with their Speeding Condition: 10 years of China's Urbanism and Architecture project, and in the second, again with Wang Jun, with their Bidding-Building (2007). He was exhibition curator of the Chinese National Library 'Regeneration Strategy: Beijing New Xisi Project International Invitation Exhibition' (2007), and co-curator, with Wei Shannon, of the New York Architecture Centre 'Building China: Five Projects, Five Stories' (2008).

Sun Shiwen is currently a professor of urban planning at Tongji University, Shanghai, from which he obtained his BE, ME and PhD degrees, all in the field of urban planning and design. His major research interests are in planning theory, urban policy study and urban planning implementation. His recent publications include: *Modern Urban Planning Theory* (China Architecture & Building Press, 2007), *The Reader in Urban Planning Regulations* (Tongji University Press, 1997/1999) and *The Philosophy of Urban Planning* (China Architecture & Building Press, 1997). He is also the author of more than 60 research papers on urban planning and design in China, and his urban planning theory has been published in numerous journals throughout the country.

Yushi Uehara has been living, and running his own practice, in the Netherlands since 1988, and runs research projects at postgraduate schools including the Berlage Institute in Rotterdam. He writes on critical architectural issues for several international architectural publications including *a+u* (Japan), *Detail* (Germany) and *Volume* (the Netherlands). He has practised in the internationally renowned offices of, for example, OMA, Toyo Ito, Kazuyo Sejima, de Architecten Cie and Daniel Libeskind, and has realised several international large-scale projects. His own practice's completed projects include the Regus Office and Elementary School in Leeuwarden. He is a winner of the Shinkenchiku residential competition.

Wang Jun is a graduate of Renmin University of China, majoring in journalism from 1987 to 1991. He then worked at the Beijing branch of the Xinhua News agency as a reporter, focusing on urban planning and construction, and is currently an editor at *Outlook Weekly* magazine. He spent more than 10 years researching and writing his first book, *Cheng Ji (Beijing Record: A Physical and Political History of Planning Modern Beijing)*, which was released in 2003. Now in its seventh edition, it has sold more than 60,000 copies in China and won numerous awards. *Cheng Ji* has also gained international exposure, including an exhibition at the East–West/North–South Program in Bordeaux, France, in 2004, and a panel discussion at a UNESCO-sponsored conference on historical preservation in 2005.

Zhang Jie is a PhD professor and doctoral students mentor at the Tsinghua University School of Architecture, Beijing. He obtained his BArch from the Architecture Department at Tianjin University, China, and PhD from the Institute of Advanced Architectural Studies, University of York. He is a visiting professor at Harvard Graduate School of Design and the Institute of Political Sciences, Paris, and a key member of the Urban Conservation Academic Committee, China Urban Planning Society, the Academic Committee of Humane Settlements and the China Architects

Society, and a member of the Urban Design Academic Committee, China Urban Planning Society. His major competition-winning projects include: conservation and renewal studies for the Furongjie historic area in the old city centre of Jinan, Shangdong Province (1996); the Fuyoujie Housing Redevelopment design, Beijing (2001); the Urban Landscape Control Master Plan for the City of Jinan (2005). Publications include: *Modern Urban Housing in China: 1840–2000* (Prestel 2001).

Zhi Wenjun was born in Shengzhou, Zhejiang Province. After graduating from Tongji College of Architecture and Urban Planning, Shanghai, he remained in Tongji and is currently a professor and researcher, and Chief Editor of *Time + Architecture* magazine. He is a director of the Shanghai Architecture Society, a member of the editorial committee of the Architecture Society of China, and Executive Director and Director of International Relations of the Shanghai Scientific Journal Association.

Zhou Rong is an associate professor at the Tsinghua University School of Architecture, Beijing, and assistant mayor of Shuozhou, Shanxi Province. He was previously a partner at FCJZ Atelier, and is currently in charge of graduate lecture courses in architectural criticism at Tsinghua University, Beijing. He is also doing theoretical research and project design in both architecture and urban design.

AD+

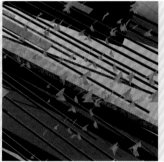

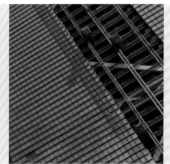

CONTENTS

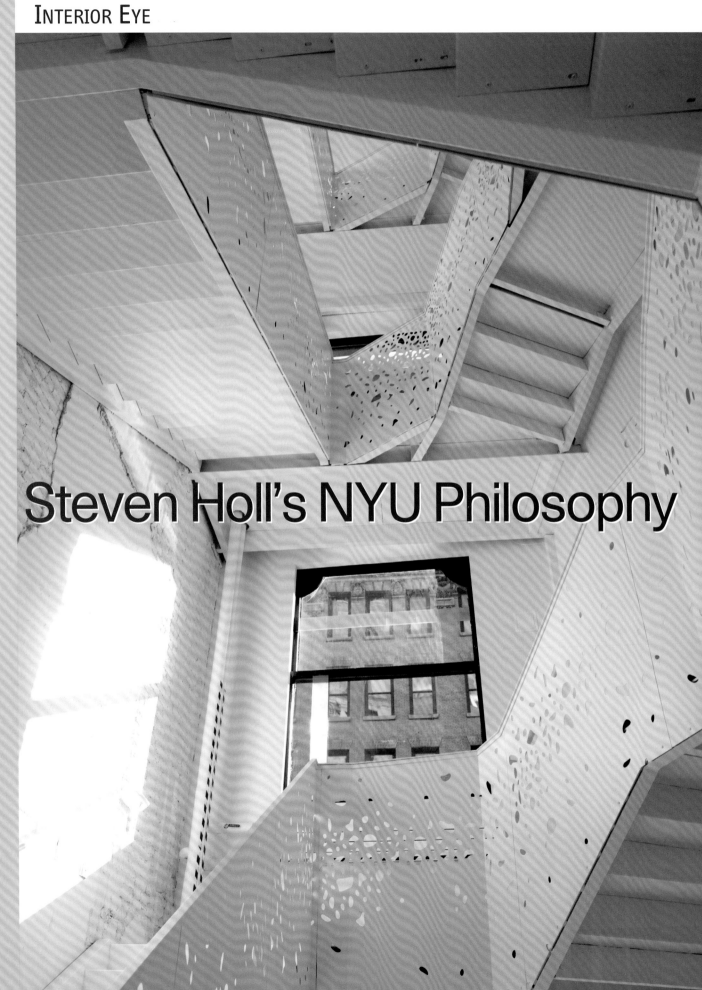

Steven Holl's NYU Philosophy

The New York University Department of Philosophy, by Steven Holl Architects, combines crisply detailed, rigidly rectangular, black and white elements with odd angles, holey walls and fluctuating rainbows inside a soft, curvaceous old masonry building with Romanesque details. Even though the architect is working on enormous mixed-use projects all over the world now, he took a special interest in creating new facilities for the philosophers close to home despite a constricted site and modest budget. Jayne Merkel describes the striking and rather mysterious new spaces in a small-floorplate, six-storey Victorian-era warehouse in Greenwich Village.

Here, an angular desk designed by the architects has been stained white; the cork floors are stained black.

Steven Holl Architects, New York University Department of Philosophy, Washington Place and Mercer Street, Greenwich Village, New York City, 2004–07
The light-filled spiralling angular staircase connects the building with dramatic shapes, broad landings and occasional flashes of colour from several-inch-wide strips of prismatic film, which cast a multicoloured of reflections on the staircase walls. Some parts of the old brick party wall are simply whitewashed. Others are covered with plaster, which is also whitewashed, giving the east wall irregular patterns as well.

Most American colleges have campuses spread over greenswards in rural villages or behind gates on the edges of cities. But NYU is housed in a loose collection of high-rise buildings, both new and historic, in densely packed Greenwich Village. A few, like the 12-storey Philip Johnson-designed Bobst Library, were built for the school, but many departments are housed in existing commercial buildings or row houses scattered throughout the neighbourhood. Philosophy shared space with other departments in a nearby building until four years ago when its faculty was offered a six-storey, brownstone and brick warehouse at the corner of Washington Place and Mercer Street, one block west of Broadway and one block east of Washington Square, surrounded by other buildings that now house university offices and classrooms.

You would think the normally sober philosophers would have been ecstatic, but they were concerned about how the department would function spread over six floors, with only half a dozen offices on each and classrooms stacked rather than lined up next to one another.

The architects solved the problem of a vertical facility by creating a wide, light-filled staircase, a 'Tower of Light', or 'backbone' of the department that spirals around at irregular angles, occasionally spreading out into deep landings that invite casual meetings. There is a new skylight overhead; the north wall is perforated to admit light from adjacent spaces; and the south wall has tall windows on each floor. The whiteness and brightness of the staircase varies with the angle and intensity of the sun, while several-inch-wide strips of prismatic film running vertically and horizontally over the window panes sometimes cast rainbows of reflections on inner staircase walls. The architects' idea, inspired by the Austrian philosopher Ludwig Wittgenstein's (1889–1951) *Remarks on Color*, was to confine themselves to black and white, and let light provide natural refractions for colour. The one exception was the ground floor where cork and ash are left unstained in their natural states.

The shape of the new staircase that the architects inserted also relates to what philosophers do – encourage one to rethink one's ideas. It changes directions and angles again and again. The structural design, developed by Nat Oppenheimer of Robert Silman structural engineers, is modelled on a simple metal pan system with 30.5-centimetre (12-inch) steel channels, but because of the complicated geometry of the large, odd-shaped landings, to prevent twisting the framing had to cross below each one and connect to the main structural members. A spider's web of steel supports is visible from below. The lower Z-shaped landings hang from steel members enclosed in the faceted stair wall. The staircase is so mesmerising that students and faculty usually take the stairs instead of the elevator – a rarity in New York. People even wander out there to chat or discuss esoteric ideas.

A casual gathering space by the entrances is framed by a perforated angled wall made of veneer-core plywood faced with plain-sliced ash veneer. The perforations were water-jet cut in patterns designed by the architects. The panels are layered on top of the 90-minute fire glass that permits views through to the staircase while achieving the required two-hour fire rating.

Perforated walls separate the lounges, meeting rooms and classrooms on the south side of each floor from the staircase on the east. This especially comfortable sixth-floor skylighted lounge can be used for seminars or social events, since it is adjacent to a kitchen and has various types of seating.

Steven Holl's personal interest in philosophy was one of the things that convinced the philosophers to hire his practice, though it probably did not hurt that he was one of the most respected architects in New York. And his reputation has soared since the celebrated opening of the addition to the Nelson-Atkins Museum of Art in Kansas City last year – a series of glass cubes distributed throughout the landscape that was praised by every critic. Now he has three huge mixed-use projects in China that are attracting interest: the 221,462-square-metre (2,383,797-square-foot) Linked Hybrid complex in Beijing, the 33,235-square-metre (357,743-square-foot) Vanke Center in Shenzhen, and the five towers of the Sliced Porosity Block in Chengdu.

All three build on the concept of porosity that Holl first used in the Sarphatistraat Offices in Amsterdam (1996–2000) where he carved away interior spaces approximating a sponge. He developed it much further at MIT's Simmons Hall dormitory, completed two years later, creating voids throughout the structure. At NYU, the white metal staircase guardrails are pierced by irregular laser-cut circular openings of different shapes and sizes, as is a bent white-ash wall between the staircase and the public spaces on each floor (with lounges of various types, casual meeting areas and classrooms).

On the ground level, where there are entrances on the corner of Washington Place and Mercer Street, the perforated wall frames a casual seating area with nine movable cubes of solid ash (designed by Brent Comber) and ash window-benches over the heating units (designed by the architects). The seating cubes even have their cracks unfilled as if the trees they come from have just been felled. The floor is natural cork tile, which is stained black upstairs. And cork is not just used for flooring; 7-millimetre (0.27-inch) thick cork panelling lines the walls of a ground-level 120-seat lecture hall, where it proved to be inexpensive, attractive and excellent for acoustics. Near the entrances, a curving ash guard-station echoes the shape of that very popular hall the philosophers share with other departments.

All furniture and office partitions on each of the 464-square-metre (5,000-square-foot) upper floors are strictly rectangular, abstract compositions made of black- or white-stained ash, or metal and glass. They contrast dramatically with the dynamic stairway and the colourful chaotic scene visible from the generous windows. The very pristine, controlled, orderly world of the philosophers looks out on the rest of the campus, but remains a very special precinct. ⊅+

The Richardson Romanesque building where the Department of Philosophy has decamped was built as a warehouse in 1890 and designed by Alfred Zucker, as were many of the buildings the university now occupies. It contains 2,787 square metres (30,000 square feet) of space on six floors. Large windows on the south and west sides fill the interiors with natural light, which is augmented by skylights on the sixth floor and over the stairwell.

The larger perforated openings on the interior of the stair are made with USG Fiberock panels with Aqua-Tough (which allows them to be laser cut and submerged in water for extended periods of time). The Fiberock works seamlessly with the gypsum wallboard nearby, which is also painted white.

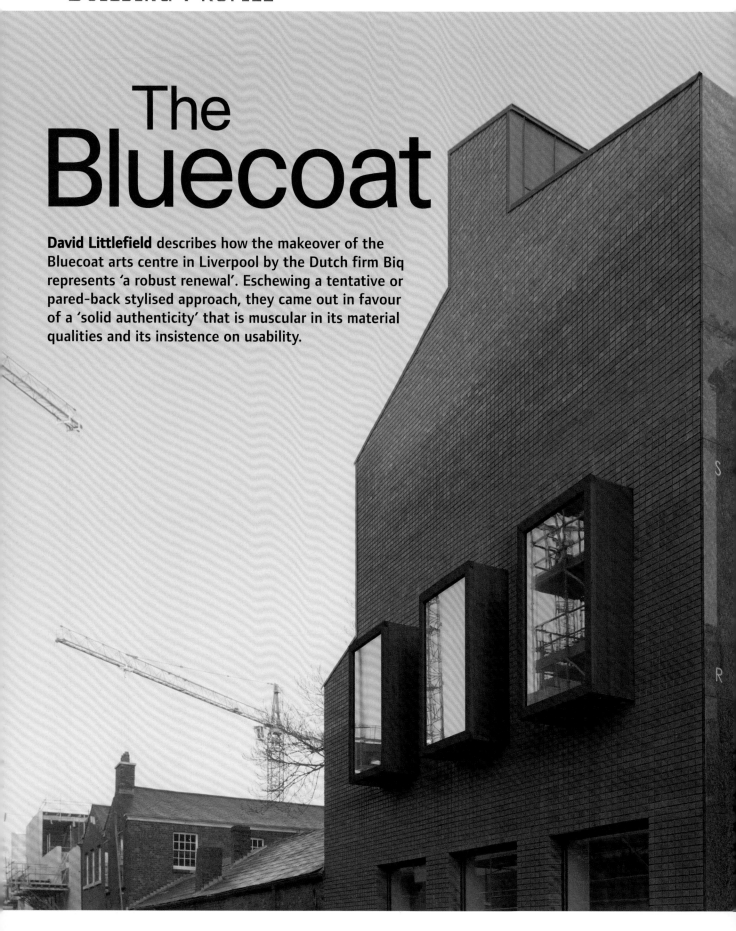

The Bluecoat

David Littlefield describes how the makeover of the Bluecoat arts centre in Liverpool by the Dutch firm Biq represents 'a robust renewal'. Eschewing a tentative or pared-back stylised approach, they came out in favour of a 'solid authenticity' that is muscular in its material qualities and its insistence on usability.

To help mark the reopening of Liverpool's Bluecoat arts centre, curators commissioned artist Janet Hodgson to make a film. The result, *Re-run*, goes a long way to summing up what this building is all about. In it, volunteers and members of staff use the building, at various phases of its reconstruction, to re-enact chase scenes from classic films (*Don't Look Now*, *The Shining*, etc). The building weighs heavily on the protagonists, and you cannot help but think it is the building itself that is the source of fear and anxiety, and which is doing the chasing. The seven-minute movie ends in the room you are actually sitting in; at the centre of the screen is the bench you are sitting on. You are implicated – you are a witness to the chases of the Bluecoat because you are there. You are there in the room where it all happened.

History has not actually been chasing Biq, the Dutch architects who have just reinvented the Bluecoat, but it has been ever present, looking over their shoulders. At the Bluecoat, history is not just an idea to which some deference is due; it is very real, solid even. The building was constructed as a school for the children of the poor in 1717. A century later a number of service buildings at the back were demolished, making way for a courtyard, and the Bluecoat's distinctive curved wall was added. In 1906 the school closed and, a year later, reopened as an arts centre. History does not end there. The building was bombed in the Second World War and the left-hand wing, as one approaches the building, is pretty much a facade only – the floorplates are of concrete, dating from the 1950s. Come the 21st century, the Bluecoat had become a muddle. There were more than 30 different floor heights in the building, while the principal performance space (formerly a chapel) was ineffective and disabled access was poor. Paying for essential works required expansion – more studios to let, more workshop space in which to run courses, bigger galleries to pull in larger crowds which, in turn, attracts greater funding.

Biq, The Bluecoat Arts Centre, Liverpool, 2008
The corner of the gallery is cut away and sheathed in granite with a Latin inscription. This facade of the building faces directly on to the city's new retail district, currently known as Liverpool One.

This atrium, of concrete and stack-bonded brick, is a surprisingly lofty space to encounter within the building. Architect Hans van der Heijden says the quality of the concrete is not as good as he imagined, but that the brickwork is better.

This arcade, with gallery space to the left and a performance hall above, is one of the most arresting places in the reinvented Bluecoat. The staircase at the end leads to a large, first-floor gallery.

This building is rough where it can afford to be, and polished where it has to be. The rear corner of the new extension has been cut away and clad in sleek, black granite with a Latin inscription; inside, the rough edge where a 20th-century wall has been ripped away has been left as a jagged scar.

Biq won the job after responding to an *OJEC* (*Official Journal of the European Communities*) advert. Although a young practice, Biq has an impressive portfolio of (largely residential) built work; this Rotterdam-based firm has done a housing scheme in Birkenhead (practice director Hans van der Heijden formerly taught architecture at the University of Liverpool). But what really won them the Bluecoat job was their approach – an unsentimental sensitivity to the building beneath the décor – and a robust, very logical, very hands-on willingness to wrestle with the building as found. Biq rejected out of hand the obvious solution, a polite makeover with deferential extension, in favour of robust renewal. Biq aimed for something very solid with its own authenticity. Before beginning design work the practice, with the Bluecoat's artistic director Bryan Biggs, hired a van and toured the country's new cultural buildings. It was their visit to Glasgow's Tramway arts centre, created from a former tram depot in 2000, that gave them the confidence they needed to take on the Bluecoat. 'Everything seemed possible,' says van der Heijden.

Van der Heijden used two approaches on the Bluecoat. First, his practice stripped the building back to its essence; second, they extruded key lines from the original building, such as the heights and rhythm of the windows, from which to plot the composition of the new works. 'We looked at the building not in conservation or historic terms, just in architectural terms. We stripped the building back to its essential form,' he says. Actually, the architects did not strip the building back entirely – they took a cool, hard look at everything and made a series of hard judgements about what should stay and what should go. An original staircase complete with scratched varnish, for example, was retained without any alterations. 'We didn't race around the building ripping everything out like idiots. But this isn't about atmospherics. It's about deadpan logic,' says van der Heijden.

It is also about creating a building you can actually use. The Bluecoat is not just an art gallery – it is also a place where practising artists rent studios and where art actually happens (Yoko Ono performed there in the 1960s, and was reprising her work here at the time of writing). The original building (scrubbed up, reworked and thoroughly modernised) has been extended with the addition of a new brick and concrete wing. The concrete walls will be drilled to receive new artworks, and when the art comes down the holes will be filled in; after many years the walls might be a patchwork of Rawlplugs and filler. 'It's very physical. This is a place where you can actually do things,' says Bluecoat chief executive Alastair Upton. Here, it is the art that is curated, not the building. There's nothing effete about the Bluecoat.

The concrete, poured *in situ*, is a pretty rough affair – it has a manhandled, patched aesthetic rather than a machined one. Van der Heijden jokes that it should be called *Béton Scouse*. In fact, the concrete is of poorer quality than the architects envisaged, although the stack-bonded brickwork is actually better, so van der Heijden is content. This building is rough where it can afford to be, and polished where it has to be. The rear corner of the new extension has been cut away and clad in sleek, black granite with a Latin inscription; inside, the rough edge where a 20th-century wall has been ripped away has been left as a jagged scar. This is a building to be touched rather than gazed at.

View into the central courtyard from within the arcade of the new extension. Unusually, galleries in this arts centre receive plentiful daylight.

The brickwork inside the new gallery is painted white, but outside materials retain their own natural colour. The roof is clad in copper.

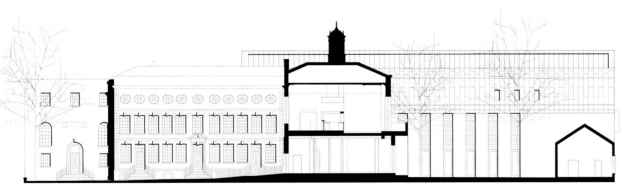

Section through the entrance block, showing the 1717 facade of one wing (left) and the new extension (right). The position and size of the extension's window openings have been drawn from the proportions of the windows on an older wing opposite.

The principal entrance to the Bluecoat. The wing on the left suffered Second World War bomb damage, and the floorplates within are of 1950s concrete.

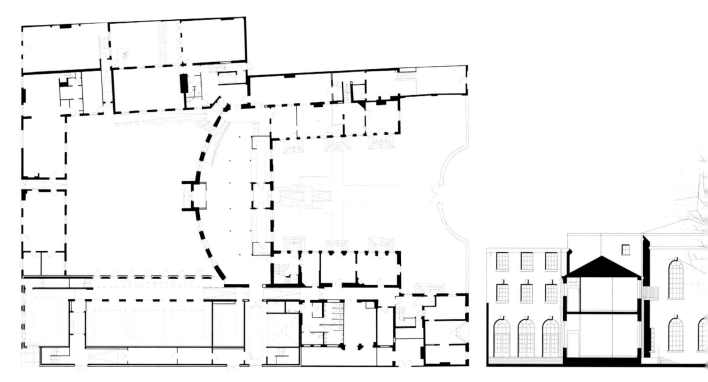

Ground-floor plan of the extended Bluecoat. The contemporary building is located along the bottom.

The central café space, formerly the main performance venue, above the entrance. The curved wall (left) overlooks the central courtyard.

There is also some rather clever planning and detailing at work. The new performance space, which can accommodate up to 240 people, is flexible enough to be used in any orientation, while the main gallery space can be subdivided into three smaller rooms as required. But this is not, of course, where the excitement lies. The thrill of this building is in discovering a large, full-height, top-lit void of brick and concrete; or in ascending the long, thin staircase which rises between vertiginous walls. Most of all, the real kick is in finding that contextualism need not put architects at a disadvantage. By responding to the clues whispered by the original building, and by answering robustly to an institution that has become used to rough handling, Biq has delivered something both authentic and worthwhile.

And, by all accounts, the people of Liverpool love it. When the Bluecoat put out a call to ask whether anyone wanted to cut the opening-day ribbon on 15 March, the response was amazing. So the Bluecoat bought hundreds of pairs of scissors and the ribbon was shredded in a single, simultaneous mass cut, including by those who brought along their own scissors. The building has been deservedly filled with people ever since. ∆+

David Littlefield is an architectural writer. He has written and edited a number of books, including *Architectural Voices: Listening to Old Buildings*, published by John Wiley & Sons (October 2007). He is also curating the exhibition 'Unseen Hands: 100 Years of Structural Engineering', which will run at the Victoria & Albert Museum until 7 September 2008. He has taught at Chelsea College of Art & Design and the University of Bath.

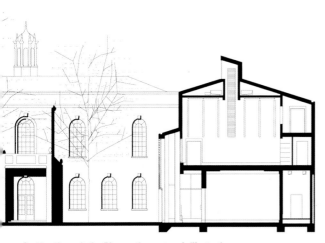

Section through the Bluecoat's courtyard, illustrating the new gallery spaces on the right.

CJ Lim/Studio 8 Architects
Through the Looking Glass

Studio 8 Architects, with CJ Lim (centre).

CJ Lim is one of architecture's greatest illustrators, visualising through his beautiful and delicate drawings and models an enchanted world inspired by Lewis Carroll, William Heath Robinson and Chinese fables. Howard Watson describes how Lim is now breaking through the visionary's glass ceiling with his realisation of a tunnel installation for the Victoria & Albert Museum in London and a project at an altogether different scale for an eco-city in China.

CJ Lim has a great affection for Lewis Carroll's tales of Alice. When he peers through the looking glass he too sees a world that is related but exceedingly different to the one we currently inhabit. However, rather than the random, topsy-turvy illogic of Wonderland, he conjures a world that has at its heart rational aesthetic solutions which belie an initially eccentric perception. This marriage between the ability to see an alternative narrative and a socially conscious, systematic, problem-solving intelligence is being revealed through a series of short-listed competition entries that are edging him towards having his visions made flesh, or at least steel and concrete. Lim, who has as yet had little built, is on the cusp of seeing his academic concepts burst out of the sketchbook and, when they do, it seems likely that they will express his unique architectural voice on a very grand scale.

A Chinese Malaysian, CJ Lim was born in Ipoh. He graduated from the Architectural Association (AA) in London in 1987 and has had teaching roles ever since at the AA, the University of North London, the University of East London and, most notably, the Bartlett, where he is Professor of Architecture + Cultural Design and Director of International Development. He studied at the AA at an interesting time, immediately following on from Nigel Coates' revolt against a prescriptive academic approach to architecture and the consequent creation of NATO (Narrative Architecture Today). He says that the greatest influence on him at the AA was Peter Salter: 'He turned everything around for me, teaching only one building, the Maison de Verre in Paris, allowing us to understand materiality, to understand the narrative through the detail.' Lim was not involved in NATO, saying: 'We were just these fresh-faced kids, and they were so confident and cool.' But he has certainly followed a sympathetic line in his own approach to both academia and architecture. He has no desire to preach his own way of seeing to his students, regarding himself as merely a guide who helps their individual creativity to blossom.

Lim was particularly interested in model-making at the AA and he continues to work in three dimensions rather than through computer programs. He has taken model-making to its own art form, incising, lifting and gluing paper to turn the one-dimensional into layered, highly illustrative building-machines that are reminiscent of William Heath Robinson, one of his heroes. His drawings/models have won a series of awards at the Royal Academy Summer Show. His narrative designs are clearly informed by his own journey from Chinese Malaysian village life to London academia, and he finds inspiration within the East–West collision of these cultures. Talking about his *Virtually Venice* project of 2004, Lim says: 'My understanding is different because of my background. Growing up in a village my understanding of habitation and so on is different from the Western city. Then I went to the AA. My whole understanding of design is in these two different worlds. Gossips, fables and tales are important in the East. Narratives, things I read in childhood, came back in this project. Architecture should be personal. The human touch is

Nam June Paik Museum, Korea, 2003
Studio 8's butterfly-attracting entry for the international competition.

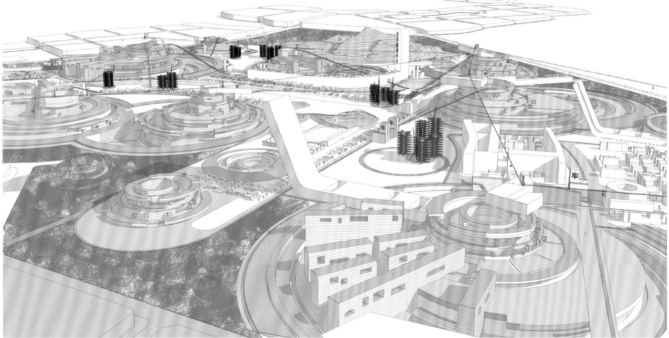

Guangming Smart-City, China, 2007

According to Lim: 'The question is how we can use social issues to make our society richer.' For the competition to design an 8-square-kilometre (3-square-mile) eco-city in Shenzhen, China, Lim addressed the problems of the local farming community to devise an ecologically sound city that would also be socially and economically sustainable, drawing on local people's skills rather than removing their livelihood. He delved into the 18th-century typologies of local communities and buildings that still exist in rural China and updated them into an integrated farming and housing environment. The concentric forms of towers and craters are inspired by traditional round community buildings and Chinese courtyard life, applying the social focus back to the centre. Lim says: 'We pursue the human story and its grittiness. Otherwise a city will be one-dimensional, like Singapore.' The concept, which includes reed-bed water filtration, lychee-tree air filtration and bio-gas public transport, was developed with Fulcrum (UK) sustainability engineers. It won third prize but the commission is potentially being divided into different sectors, with Studio 8 designing a large area.

essential.' He humbly says that 'As much as I want to contribute to the built environment, I hope I have already contributed a bit to architecture,' but the challenge for Lim is to lift his ideas off the paper to make them take a solid form. He can draw optimism from the success of Zaha Hadid, a fellow alumna from the AA, who has been able to take her pictorial imagination into a successful but still visionary practice. Lim does talk of his need 'to build to test the narrative', and that is where Studio 8 Architects comes in.

He formed Studio 8 Architects in London in 1994 and was immediately successful, winning the University College London Cultural Centre competition the following year. If that building had come to fruition, Lim's career would have taken a different turn, but economic restraints left the project in abeyance. Undeterred, Studio 8 continued to pursue international competitions for cultural buildings, including for the Jyväskylä Centre in Finland and the Tomohiro Museum of Shi-Ga in Japan. The 2003 entry for the Nam June Paik Museum in Korea reveals Lim's desire to create narratives that relate to him but simultaneously respond to a building's purpose and its topography. Inspired by Nam June Paik's own artworks,

the building followed the undulation of the earth and was crowned by cantilevered glass pavilions. The glass was to be protected by louvres made from the trees that would be felled to make way for the building, while parts of the building's exterior skin would feature tiny pipettes secreting a sugar solution. The surrounding park area has hordes of butterflies which would be attracted to the sugar and form a fluttering wave on the building, reminiscent of Paik's *TV Garden* of 120 television monitors flickering among a garden of plants. The project showed that Studio 8 was leaning towards a passion for cultural and environmental sustainability that would be borne out in their more recent, large-scale works.

Alongside the competition entries, CJ Lim has blurred the boundaries between architecture and art in a series of personal projects. *Sins*, of 2000, was a seven-part project partly inspired by *Se7en*, the David Fincher film, and showed the diversity of the architect's interests and inspirations. One of the projects, 'The Jerry Springer Museum: Kiss and Tell', explored the modern concept of the celebration of confession, allowing people to tell their stories in public confessional booths. The whispered revelations would then be relayed to a listening space where people could eavesdrop, forming an undulating, endlessly changing environment.

The genre of competition entries for public architecture and his artistic leanings came together within Lim's design for the Mersey Observatory, Liverpool, in 2008. His unusual, highly sculptural, V-shaped ribbon was

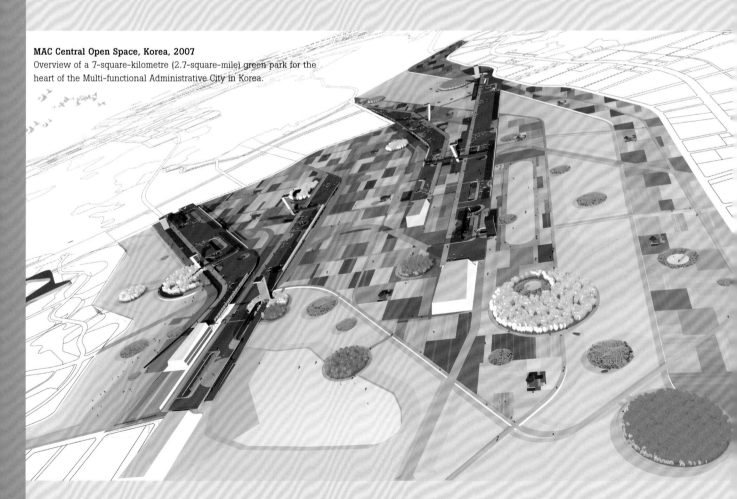

MAC Central Open Space, Korea, 2007
Overview of a 7-square-kilometre (2.7-square-mile) green park for the heart of the Multi-functional Administrative City in Korea.

Mersey Observatory, Liverpool, 2008
Finalist for the competition for a viewing platform in Liverpool.

Lim's narrative-inspired architectural artworks have culminated in *Seasons Through the Looking Glass*, an installation piece that was commissioned for the underground tunnel entrance to the Victoria & Albert Museum in London. This is a large artwork that draws on *Alice's Adventures in Wonderland* to explore the possibilities of mythical underground spaces and subterranean gardens.

Seasons Through the Looking Glass,
Victoria & Albert Museum, London, 2008

Inspired by the tunnel setting for an installation commissioned by the
Victoria & Albert Museum, Lim drew on the story of *Alice's Adventures in
Wonderland,* written by Lewis Carroll in 1865, in which Alice falls
through a tunnel into another world. The rose garden of the story, in
which gardeners paint the petals of the roses, is reborn as a cartouche-
shaped structure made of honeycomb cardboard. The roses are rolled-up
white T-shirts pinioned within the branches. The installation will
change with the seasons, becoming splashed with coloured vinyl paint.
Situated at the underground entrance to the museum, the work evokes
the mysteries of the subterranean while reflecting the role of the
museum in housing crafted objects and highlighting the wonder of
crossing into a new world. The passing public is drawn into the V&A
tunnel by an Alice-inspired mirror (or 'looking glass') of the installation
in the main tunnel which links several major museums. Lim often draws
upon books, fairy tales and films for inspiration, saying: 'I have been
lucky to go through many metamorphoses of what I like and respond to.
This has stimulated me and given me new challenges.'

Virtually Venice, Venice Biennale, 2004

For the Venice Biennale of 2004, the British Council commissioned Lim
to create an extensive new work. He was inspired by the story of the
13th-century friendship formed between Marco Polo and the Mongol
emperor Kublai Khan. Polo used to tell the emperor stories of his travels,
including tales from his homeland of Venice. Lim's narrative, informed
by his own journey from East to West, portrays Venice as it may have
been imagined by Kublai Khan, translating Polo's descriptions through
an occidental lens. He created a range of paper models reimagining the
eight water towers of the Fortuna Pozzo-Pozza, San Michele, as a place
of rest, and the Giardini as an area textured by foreign languages and
information exchange. Lim used paper for the construction as it was the
cutting-edge technology of the era.

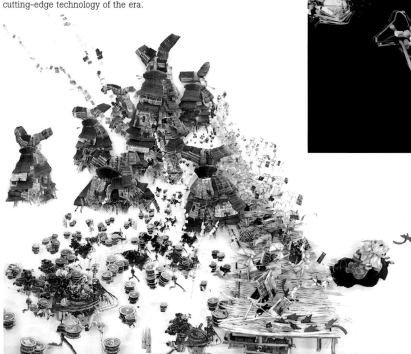

to cantilever over the broad River Mersey, forming an observation deck 33 metres (108.3 feet) above the water. The sculpture would include LED lighting to illuminate the V-shape at night. The short-listed design managed to incorporate the desire for something that looked upon Liverpool within a building that would be looked upon in its own right, while also carrying its visitors to a closer relationship with the city's historically important river. CJ Lim's ability to match his radical vision with the requirements of a competition has recently resulted in Studio 8 being short-listed for seven of ten competition entries.

Lim's narrative-inspired architectural artworks have culminated in *Seasons Through the Looking Glass*, an installation piece that was commissioned for the underground tunnel entrance to the Victoria & Albert Museum in London. This is a large artwork that draws on *Alice's Adventures in Wonderland* to explore the possibilities of mythical underground spaces and subterranean gardens. In Lewis Carroll's novel, Alice falls through a tunnel into another world, in which she sees gardeners painting the flowers of a rose garden. Lim's cardboard structure, with delineated branches holding rolled-up white T-shirts/roses, manages to emphasise the tunnel environment, artistic craft (the *raison d'être* of the V&A) and the wonder of crossing the threshold into a museum experience. The V&A has become a collector of Lim's works and has included his Guangming Smart-City design, a project on an altogether different scale, in its 2008 'China Design Now' exhibition.

The Guangming design was predated by another vast urban design that Lim created when he was selected to be part of the Peter Cook-curated show in the British Pavilion at the Venice Architecture Biennale of 2004. *Virtually Venice* manages to be both a personal and large-scale evocation of the essence of Lim's approach. His own East-West journey influences the project, which is inspired by the friendship of Kublai Khan and Marco Polo. During his 20-year stay in China, the Italian Polo would tell the Mongol emperor stories of his homeland: *Virtually Venice* is Khan's imaginary Venice as evoked through Polo's tales. The result is a startling collision of East–West narratives, filled with humour and relying on Lim's extraordinary illustrative model-making to tell the story. Since *Virtually Venice*, Studio 8 has moved towards designing large sections of sustainable urban environments. These have a precedent in his *How Green is Your Garden?* experimental research project of 2000–03, which formulated the question of whether buildings can learn from organic systems.

Lim's designs for a new Chinese eco-city in Guangming won him third prize in the international competition but the jury has now asked him to design a large section of urban park for the city. The design, which forced Studio 8's fluid team to expand from three to 15, centres on the creation of clusters of integrated housing/farming towers and craters, along with 80 vertical kitchen farms. The circular forms are drawn from the traditional Chinese model of round community buildings and courtyard living. Each element of the design carries through a deep, thorough exploration of future-city sustainability. The brief is for a green city so Studio 8 has pursued innovative ideas to recycle materials and create renewable energy sources, cut pollution, increase green space and pedestrianisation, and rely on local produce.

However, the Guangming design steps way beyond a purely eco-rationale of sustainability. Lim has been able to move up from smaller projects, in which the narrative can be more linearly relayed, into huge projects because he persists with the human scale: 'Narratives, culture and history are the strategic starting points for any project – thinking small. The way we live is interesting. I think about occupancy and intimacy.' As a result, Guangming is historically and socially sustainable as well as eco-friendly. The Guangming area supplies vegetables and dairy produce to Shenzhen and Hong Kong, so the new city will draw on the existing reality of the life of farmers, giving them a model that they can understand while also pushing them forward into a new arena of possibilities: effectively, the urban environment becomes a great food-producing garden. As Lim says about the local populace: 'We can get them to live in a modern house, but the thing that they really know is farming. There is no point in being unemployed in a modern apartment, without any skills that can be used in the city.' The name 'Smart-City' shows his intent to make sure that the failures of Modernist urban environments are not unwittingly integrated into the bravura of new eco-city design.

Guangming Smart-City has been quickly followed by other Eastern urban park designs. Studio 8's design for the Tangshen Earthquake Memorial Park in China won second prize with a calm, nature-inspired memorial to absence, while MAC Central Open Space, in Korea, pushes forward a desire to create a new urban typology, the arable kitchen garden-park, in which open-air leisure activities, orchards, watercourses and technology are integrated in a redefinition of urban parkland.

Currently, Studio 8 is a small but fluid practice with powerful ideas. Increasingly, juries are beginning to see that its outlandish, ebullient concepts are feasible, aesthetically inspiring creations that take into account logistics, the environment and social sustainability. It seems that the world is finally starting to catch up with Lim's ideas. It is highly likely that soon one of his visions is going to be given the green light and Studio 8 is going to have to rapidly expand into a permanently large practice. One can only hope that this will not dilute the pioneering thought that is the practice's foundation. *Δ+*

Howard Watson is an author, journalist and editor based in London. He is co-author, with Eleanor Curtis, of the new 2nd edition of *Fashion Retail* (Wiley-Academy, 2007), £34.99. See www.wiley.com. Previous books include *The Design Mix: Bars, Cocktails and Style* (2006), and *Hotel Revolution: 21st-Century Hotel Design* (2005), both also published by Wiley-Academy.

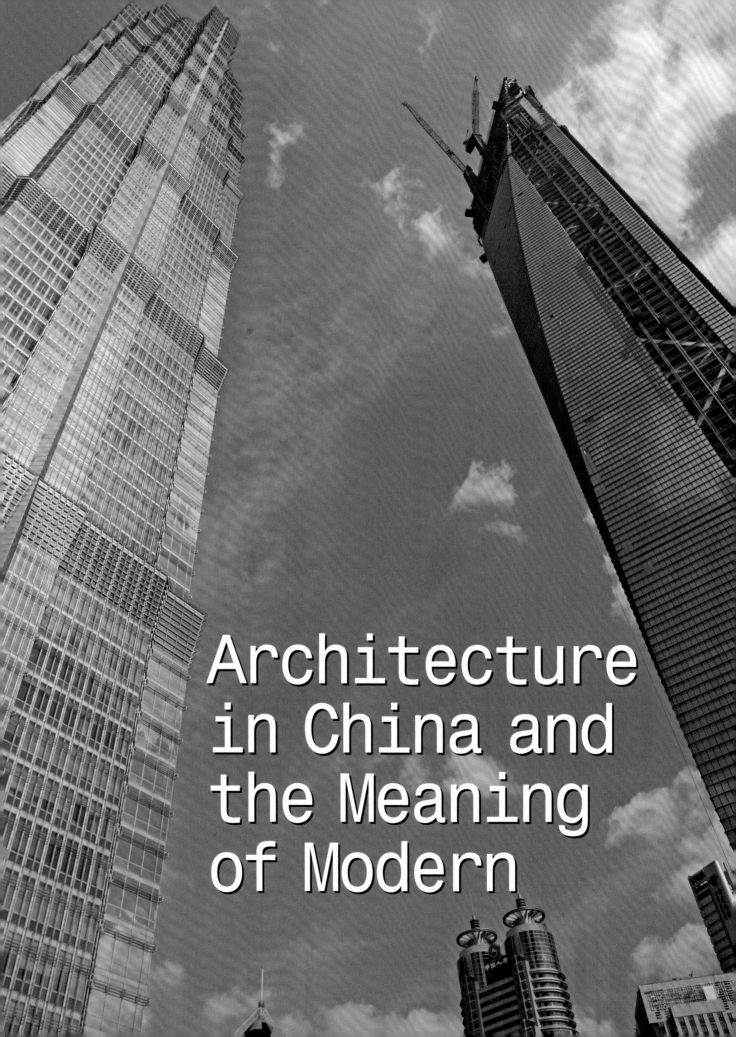

Architecture in China and the Meaning of Modern

What is generally understood by Modern architecture in China is set to be re-evaluated across the world with a major exhibition this summer at the RIBA in London and a significant new book by Edward Denison and Guang Yu Ren. Here co-author and co-curator of *Modernism in China*, **Edward Denison**, outlines why we need to look back to China's Modernist roots in the early 20th century if we are to understand the intense modernisation of the present.

It has been observed that China's architecture 'is in a state of transition and time alone can show the ultimate outcome'.[1] For a country which, until the early 20th century, proudly boasted the longest continuous architectural traditions humankind has witnessed and which, in the early 21st century, is undergoing the most extensive urban development humankind has witnessed, this observation appears decidedly understated, but since it was penned in the 1920s the author can be forgiven. What China has been through over the past century is nothing short of staggering when compared with any other perceived norm in architecture and urban planning, and yet this transition is still under way.

In this light Chinese architects might also be forgiven for struggling to reconcile the past with the present and future. Seeking to define, let alone retain, the essential qualities of their nation's architecture or hoping to sustain any form of cultural meaning in an industry that has not only been revolutionised but today bears little or no resemblance to that which preceded it just a century ago, is daunting indeed. At the dawn of the 21st century, the world appears mesmerised by China's urban growth and its apparently modern, nay futuristic, representation, but only one century ago China had no formally trained architects and relied instead on the master craftsman and builder to erect buildings in a manner passed down through a direct lineage extending, some argue, five millennia.

Shanghai's much panegyrised futuristic skyline.

In architecture, such time scales confound Western minds to the point of losing their meaning. In the West, architecture is founded largely on classical precedents that appear positively infantile in comparison to China's ancient traditions. Small wonder the French philosopher Voltaire proclaimed in the 18th century: 'Many of the learned of our northern climes have felt confounded at the antiquity claimed by the Chinese.' However, China's apparently unprecedented experiences in the 21st century belie a modernising process lasting several centuries, throughout which East and West have engaged in a fascinating dialogue and China's architecture and design in the eyes of the West has enjoyed both renown and disdain, in that order but in unequal measure.

This dialogue began in the 16th and 17th centuries with the arrival of the first European traders and Jesuit missionaries, but it was not until China was forcibly opened to international trade following the signing of the Treaty of Nanjing between Britain and China in 1842 that the country's architectural modernisation assumed an altogether different tempo. Since then, 'foreign' in the eyes of Chinese has been synonymous with 'modern', even when manifested in the form of a faux-Tudor residence, a Neoclassical bank, neo-Gothic church or neo-Baroque theatre. Although foreign architecture, construction techniques and materials penetrated China through its growing number of treaty ports in the late 19th century, and challenged the time-honoured domestic architecture characterised by the wooden frame and distinctive roof, the advent of Modernism in Europe and America from the early 20th century introduced a paradoxical twist to what otherwise seemed to be a steady process of architectural subjugation in which Western architectural theory and practice was wholly supplanting Eastern.

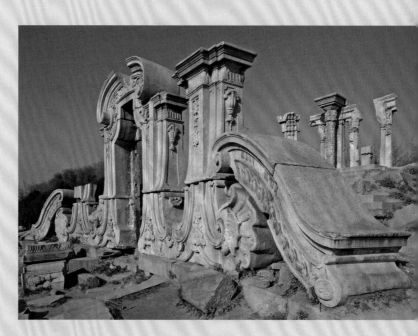

The ruins of the Jesuit buildings in Beijing's Yuan Ming Yuan gardens, built in the 18th century.

Sir William Chambers' Great Pagoda,
Kew Gardens, 1762, inspired by his
well-documented admiration for
Chinese design.

The wooden frame of a Chinese
building (in this case part of the
Suzhou Museum) 'where the walls
are screens and not supports'.

This paradox was noted by a number of foreign and Chinese architects at the time, but has since been lost by subsequent written accounts of architectural history that overlooked China altogether and consequently erased the world's most populous country and its impressive architectural contributions from 20th-century historiography. Liang Si Cheng, one of China's foremost architectural minds of the last century, claimed that 'the characteristic of Chinese architecture, in terms of structure, is to build the frame first, then put up the walls and fix the windows.'[2] Though not claiming to be profound or original, this observation explains the basic principle distinguishing traditional forms of Chinese and Western architecture. But it is this characteristic, as one foreign observer noted in 1919, that was 'actually the precursor of modern building where the pillars are replaced by concrete or steel, and where the walls are screens and not supports'.[3] Therefore, while Modernists in the West embraced and rigorously promoted the freedom offered by the steel and concrete frame, their radical gospel appeared conceptually far less drastic to that of their Chinese counterparts.

However, China never fully rose to the occasion and only the era's most exceptional architects came close to articulating it in physical actuality. The Chinese architects who spent much of their professional careers grappling with these issues were China's 'first generation' of formally trained architects. Returning from foreign universities from the 1910s onwards, they formed the backbone of China's subsequent architectural community which, by the 1930s, had matured to such an extent as to challenge the previously overwhelming supremacy of foreign architects in China and win contracts to design what were at the time some of the most important buildings and urban plans in China. Central to many of these projects, and at the heart of themes running through most professional debates, was how Chinese architecture could retain any sense of meaning in an age dominated by modernity. One of the first Chinese commentators to voice concerns about this was William Chaund, who wrote of architecture in China in 1919:

Truly there has never been a time when the people at large were more determined to learn from the Occident in order to emulate them … However profoundly influenced by the western attitude and thought we must work out our own salvation … the architecture of the western world cannot be imposed upon the East without being radically modified … inherent good taste and aesthetic ideal cannot be imported like an exact science … while we admire the western achievements we should not imitate them slavishly.[4]

The urge to find appropriate expression for this radical modification caused one eminent architect, Tong Jun, two decades later to conclude: 'How to create a building in China, planned and constructed in the foreign way, with a "native" appearance, is a problem taxing the brain of Chinese architects.'[5] The predominant means by which modification was sought was through appearance; the building's style not its substance. China is thus punctuated with buildings designed by Chinese architects and constructed from the 1920s onwards that attempted to impart a sense of 'Chineseness' only through ornamentation, while neglecting or failing to explore anything more meaningful.

The most common device used to achieve this was the idiosyncratic roof, which Tong Jun viewed as 'a handy crib' used by architects to give their 'design some sort of 'face-lifting'.[6] But as Ino Dan, an assistant professor at Tokyo University, postulated when reflecting on the 2-metre (6.5-foot) deep eaves of Japanese buildings caused by the complex roof structure (an architectural element imported from China during the Tang dynasty – AD 618–907): 'The eaves may be constructed with iron

The former library in Shanghai's former Civic Centre, built in the mid-1930s, illustrating the often-criticised Chinese roof used to adorn modern structures to give them local 'meaning'.

skeleton concrete, but it is not difficult to imagine how unpleasant this would be when one realises that such a projection of roof would be made of ponderous concrete.'[7]

Nevertheless, while the materials and craftsmanship so essential to the form and character of a Chinese roof were replaced by steel and concrete, the appearance lingered unconvincingly cast in unwieldy materials, confirming Ino Dan's assertion that 'any attempt to restore the form of Japanese or Chinese architecture by means of iron and concrete should not be permitted under any circumstances',[8] though it is only fair to mention also his caveat that 'that there [was] something quite modern in its spirit'.[9] Tong Jun echoed Dan's sentiments when scorning the fundamental incompatibility of the traditional roof and the modern building, claiming that 'it would be at once an anachronism and a fallacy if the tile-roof is made to cover constructions of any size with modern interior arrangement'.[10]

However, though these efforts to fuse to two distinct architectures through style alone appear curious or even dishonest in retrospect, their rationale was founded on a concern for the loss of the country's architectural heritage at the hands of foreign influences, and fuelled by a pervasive sense of nationalism. According to the writer who penned the Foreword to the first edition of the popular Chinese architectural journal *The Builder* in 1932, if architects use only 'foreign currency', they would be 'throwing away the essence of our culture [which] will be the death of us. Thousands of years of methods of building grand palaces and elegant gardens would all be brushed aside, causing us to forget our roots and would result in a general "barbarianization". Even using foreign materials would lead to the abandonment of local products that would leave no chance of survival.'[11]

This reluctance, some might say inability, to cast aside the more superficial aspects of traditional architecture reflects a deeper dichotomy. On the one hand, the general trend for modernity led to an espousal of all things foreign, manifested in numerous examples of

classical as well as Modern structures designed by Chinese architects, while on the other there were consistent efforts to retain Chinese characteristics, often by the same architects. While the failure of the latter to achieve any true meaning proved its ultimate undoing, the former persists to this day and is one of the key drivers behind the nature of China's resurgence since the 1980s. As in the early 20th century, to pursue the foreign is to pursue the modern.

On a grand scale, this finds expression in city planning, such as Shanghai's Pudong District from the early 1990s. China looked overseas for guidance before finally creating its own design from a ruinous attempt to combine the four separate proposals submitted by some of the world's leading architectural firms. On a smaller scale, this also finds expression in the much-criticised themed suburbs surrounding cities such as Shanghai, designed as kitsch fantasy worlds in the vernacular style of a range of foreign countries. But it is on the scale of the individual building that this finds its most obvious and pervasive expression. A key ingredient in China's

architectural resurgence since the 1980s has been the iconic structure with the prerequisite foreign architect's name tag. So common now are these structures that their currency has been greatly devalued, along with, some would argue, the reputations of the foreign architects responsible for creating them in the first place. With some notable exceptions, it is a classic case of quantity not quality, but the demand among municipalities all over China for their cities to host such creations remains strong because the policy has transcended architecture and become as much an exercise in branding as an affirmation of arrival into a modern world.

Meanwhile, these structures, very few of which might truly be adjudged to be iconic by any international measure, are, like those designed by their forebears, slavishly reproduced by Chinese architects working in an industry that offers very little in the way of creative incentives so that cityscapes like Shanghai today may boast their tally of 4,000 high-rise buildings constructed in little over 15 years. This reverberates with the comments of one leading Chinese architect, Doon Da You, who said in 1936 of the state of architecture in China that 'the buildings put up were merely poor imitations of European models with the exteriors only a shade more hideous than the interior'.[12]

Thames Town in Shanghai's western suburbs; one of many themed suburbs built in recent years based on the vernacular architecture of various European countries.

The former villa of Sun Ke (1948) and the former offices of the China Merchants Steam Navigation Company (1947), both in Nanjing, designed by Yang Ting Bao in a Modern style, but with evident Chinese characteristics, especially in plan.

However, it is here that there can be found ample cause for optimism. Now, as occurred at the end of China's previous era of architectural exuberance, a small number of architects are seeking deeper meaning in their work, suggestive of what Ino Dan coined the 'spirit' of Asia's distinct architecture, and it is with this group that an evident creativity appears distinct from China's hugely standardised architectural industry. It is perhaps too early to name these contemporary architects, but enough time has passed since the 1930s and 1940s to identify a similar group of distinguished architects who expressed a desire to move beyond the mere reproduction of foreign trends; and evidenced in their most accomplished work is a notable success in resolving Chinese tradition and modernity. Liang Si Cheng, Tong Jun (one of the partners of the renowned Chinese firm Allied Architects), and Doon Da You have already been mentioned, but there are a number of others, prominent among whom is Yang Ting Bao, a graduate of the University of Pennsylvania, classmate of Louis Kahn, and exceptional student.

This conspicuous minority successfully overcame the red herring of ornamentation and, understanding that 'the Chinese builder never sacrificed the structure for any decoration, however attractive',[13] produced some of the best work in China that successfully married tradition and modernity before the advent of communism opened an entirely new chapter in the nation's architectural history. If history is anything to go by, it might just be that a similarly experienced group of Chinese architects are now emerging to challenge a similar foreign dominance in China. If so, like their forebears, it is with them that Chinese architecture might be raised from its lowly position, where it has remained since its unceremonious relegation in the minds of the West, when foreigners started exerting a strong influence in China from the 19th century. ∆+

Edward Denison and Guang Yu Ren are specialists in the field of the built environment, with a particular focus on cultural heritage and development. Their work is regularly featured in publications and broadcast media, and at international symposia. As well as *Modernism in China*, their co-authored publications include *Asmara: Africa's Secret Modernist City* (Merrell 2003 and 2007) and *Building Shanghai: The Story of China's Gateway* (Wiley Academy, 2006 and 2007). These works form the basis of two travelling exhibitions that continue to disseminate these unique subjects to audiences as far apart as Europe, the Middle East, Africa and America.

'Modernism in China' is showing in Gallery 1 at the RIBA, London, between 3 July and 27 September 2008. See www.architecture.com. Edward Denison and Guang Yu Ren, *Modernism in China*, is published by John Wiley & Sons, see www.wiley.com.

Notes

1. J Van Wie Bergamini, 'Architectural Meditations', *The Chinese Recorder*, October 1924, p 650.
2. Liang Si Cheng, 'Suggestions on the Location of the Administrative Center of the Central People's Government, February 1950', with Chen Zhan Xiang, *Collection of Liang Si Cheng's Writing*, Vol 4, China Architectural Industry Publisher, September, 1986.
3. Gerald King, 'The Utilisation of Chinese Architecture Design in Modern Building – the Rockefeller Foundation's Hospital Plant at Peking, *Far Eastern Review*, Vol 15, August 1919, p 562.
4. William Chaund, 'Architectural Effort and Chinese Nationalism – Being a Radical Interpretation of Modern Architecture as a Potent Factor in Civilisation, Armour Institute of Technology, Department of Architecture', *Far Eastern Review*, Vol 15, August 1919, p 533.
5. Tong Jun, 'Architecture Chronicle', *T'ien Hsia*, Vol V, No 5, October 1937, p 308.
6. Ibid.
7. Ino Dan, 'Reconstruction of Tokyo and Aesthetic Problems of Architecture', *Far Eastern Review*, Vol 28, January 1932, p 39.
8. Ibid, p 43.
9. Ibid.
10. Tong Jun, op cit.
11. *The Builder*, No 11, 1932.
12. Doon Da You, 'Architecture Chronicle', *T'ien Hsia*, Vol 3, No 4, November 1936, p 358.
13. Tong Jun, 'Foreign Influence in Chinese Architecture', *T'ien Hsia*, Vol VI, No 5, May 1938, p 410.

Light Between Architecture and Event

Lighting conventionally provides buildings with much-needed luminescence and ambience. **Valentina Croci** investigates the work of Cologne-based practice LightLife whose lighting projects provide the very media of installations and whose schemes inject new life into neglected areas of the city. Often shifting our experiences of public and urban spaces, their projects also emphasise and extend social use.

LightLife, Linie 03, 'Blaue Nacht', Nuremberg, 2006
The climax of the installation was a series of structures in the market square: three 5-metre (16.4-foot) high cylinders with a steel pipe structure and plastic tile cladding. A computer program controlled the composition of text and graphic effects. The use of a wireless LAN system eliminated exposed wiring, increasing the safety of the installation. The event was visited by more than 130,000 people.

LightLife, Digital Movies, Voges + Deisen Gallery, Frankfurt, 2006
The gallery space was filled with curved walls and suspended lighting fixtures. Each panel was composed of 125 tiles, with 64 separately controllable RGB pixels (a red, green and blue colour-mixing system). The panels allowed for the creation of dynamic patterns and different colours of light in relationship to the number of visitors in the space as monitored by sensors located at the gallery entrance.

Architectural lighting represents an important interdisciplinary field of design. It does not end with a simple technical study, but focuses on the collaboration between different fields of expertise – architecture, engineering, urban design and computer programming – to create spaces with an emotional impact. Architectural lighting takes advantage of the dynamic and chromatic potentials of light, together with new technologies of computerised control, to create environments that are animated by human presence. This field of design has produced, above all, temporary installations for fairs, cultural and sporting events, or business communication. However, as can be seen in the work of the studio LightLife, architectural lighting is also capable of offering a service, it can be applied to private and public signage, or create opportunities for breathing new life into neglected areas of the city.

Antonius Quodt founded LightLife Gesellschaft für Audiovisuelle Erlebnisse in Cologne in 1996. The practice currently employs six full-time professional and eight freelance designers, with skills in architectural and lighting design, computer programming, acoustic design and video technologies. The office also specialises in the development of computer programs applied to dynamic environmental lighting, collaborating with e:cue (a leading company in lighting control software development). Quodt's background is in the field of radio and television broadcasting, and concert and theatre stage design. Before founding LightLife, he worked with such lighting design studios as ShowTec and Vari-Lite. LightLife's projects are the result of close collaborations with architects and artists, including Keith Sonnier, with whom the office completed the RWE-Meteorite Park in Essen (1998), and André Hellers, with whom LightLife built the 17.8-metre (58.4-foot) diameter globe for the 2006 FIFA World Cup.

Architectural lighting is both the coordination of visual and sound elements that transform space and a process for involving the public. Digital Movies, created for 'Luminale 2006' at the Voges + Deisen Gallery, Frankfurt, is an installation composed of a cylindrical access tunnel and a central space filled with a series of curved LED panels. The movement of light and sound inside the tunnel created a sensation of estrangement, an effect similar to that of a depressurisation chamber. The tunnel was connected to a large hall filled with a series of panels that generated a dynamic lighting effect, with scrolling text, including Marc Cousins' quote: 'Life is difficult enough already without art.' The lighting patterns on the walls and the sound environment were not pre-programmed, but rather created by software connected to sensors located at the entrance that controlled the presence of visitors. The installation was thus rendered interactive by its reliance on the movement and presence of the public. However, it was above all a 'happening', because the creation of the light effects by the software is unique to a given moment in time.

LightLife also developed a multimedia installation, Linie 03, for the 2006 'Blaue Nacht' event in Nuremberg. These annual events represent an opportunity to promote the image of the city, its services and cultural offerings. LightLife created a scenographic work to be located in public urban spaces, opening a dialogue between visitors and the city. The connecting theme was that of the colour blue (from the 'Blaue Nacht' title of the event). The city's brief stipulated that the installation was to be used to publicise the event programme. LightLife thus designed a series of 5-metre (16.4-foot) high display screens located near the Museum für Kommunikation and a 3.2-kilometre (2-mile) long path that terminated in three cylinders located in the market square. The structures were composed of aluminium tubes and plastic tiles, built especially for the event, with integrated lighting fixtures.

Each featured an autonomous and individually operable lighting system to create text and graphic effects, and visitor participation was ensured by allowing the public to submit messages to be broadcast on the screens.

Linie 03 thus creates interesting perspectives in the fields of public event design and different ways of using urban spaces. A similar project is Kubik, an outdoor bar composed of modular elements assembled in Berlin along the banks of the Spree River (2006), in Barcelona during the Sonar Festival (2007) and in Lisbon for the Trienal de Arquitectura (2007). Kubik is composed of 144 stackable plastic tanks mounted on steel panels. Each element incorporates standard 150W lamps, coloured filters and digital dimmers that control light intensity and energy consumption. This type of technology is neither complex nor costly, allowing Kubik to be assembled with different forms and in any outdoor context, generating a serial approach to the design of architectural lighting. The project also allows for a renewed focus on abandoned areas of the city through specific and low-budget interventions. The importance of this project was summed up by one of Kubik's visitors: 'One feels strangely secure in this brightened space with an open view to the sky.'

LightLife, Kubik, Spree Riverbank, Berlin, 2006
The particular nature of Kubik is its simple, low-cost technology and modularity. The elements can be assembled in different forms and adapted to any outdoor environment or entertainment-related activity in an urban context, making Kubik a concept-bar that can be exported to different cities. The system was developed with the architectural office Modulorbeat.

LightLife, Trading Hall, Deutsche Börse, Frankfurt, 2008
The upper part of the large two-storey trading hall is covered by a map of the world composed of fluorescent lighting tubes. The spaces between the tubes are filled with LED plaques that present real-time information from stock markets around the world. The perimeter of the room features a 1.2 metre (3.9-foot) high continuous panel that presents stock market information. The upper level features a public gallery.

The visitors' gallery is filled with interactive information columns and a digital floor that converts the commercial values of the Xetra (Exchange Electronic Trading) system into graphic patterns.

One of LightLife's most recent projects is the restyling of the Deutsche Börse in Frankfurt (2008). The project was focused, on the one hand, on the functional illumination of the stock market's working environment and, on the other, on adding a theatrical touch to the events that take place inside the building: the brokers' desks were transformed into glowing ellipses, while the upper part of the two-storey trading hall was covered with a map of the world created using fluorescent lighting tubes. The spaces between the tubes are occupied by LED plaques that present real-time information from stock markets around the world. The spaces reserved for visitors were fitted out with interactive information columns and a digital floor that translates the commercial values of the Xetra (Exchange Electronic Trading) system into graphic patterns.

This intervention is just one example of how lighting installations can be permanently inserted in everyday working environments. Lighting, together with graphics or environmental sound design, has the potential to emphasise social rituals and offer a different experience of the spaces in which they take place. ⚙+

Translated from the Italian version into English by Paul David Blackmore

Valentina Croci is a freelance journalist of industrial design and architecture. She graduated from Venice University of Architecture (IUAV), and attained an MSc in architectural history from the Bartlett School of Architecture, London. She achieved a PhD in industrial design sciences at the IUAV with a theoretical thesis on wearable digital technologies.

The restyling of the Frankfurt Stock Exchange was completed in collaboration with Stuttgart's Atelier Brückner architectural office. The windowless central room features ceiling-mounted lighting fixtures that give a daylighting effect. The brokers' desks were designed as glowing ellipses that change colour and intensity throughout the day.

Ecomasterplanning

Best known as the pioneer of the green skyscraper, Ken Yeang is now applying his innovative, ecological thinking to the urban masterplan. Here he outlines how the introduction of an ecoinfrastructure can bring multiple benefits to a city, encouraging connectivity between green spaces, providing natural habitats for wildlife and alleviating the impact of climate change by offsetting CO_2 emissions.

Ecomasterplanning is the seamless and environmentally benign integration of four strands of infrastructures: the green infrastructure (linked greenways and habitats), the grey infrastructure (the engineering infrastructure and sustainable engineering systems), the blue infrastructure (the sustainable urban drainage system), and the red, or human, infrastructure (being its built systems, hardscapes and regulatory systems).

The Green Infrastructure

The green infrastructure is the 'ecoinfrastructure' that is vital to every masterplan. This ecoinfrastructure parallels the usual 'grey' urban infrastructure of roads, drainage systems and utilities. This is an interconnected network of natural areas and other open spaces that conserves natural ecosystem values and functions, and sustains clean air and water. It also enables the area to flourish as a natural habitat for a wide range of wildlife, and delivers a wide array of benefits to humans and the natural world alike, such as providing a linked habitat across the landscape that permits bird and animal species to move freely. This ecoinfrastructure is nature's functioning infrastructure (parallel to our human-made infrastructures, designated as 'grey', 'blue' and 'red' infrastructures here), and in addition to providing cleaner water and enhancing water supplies, it can also result in some, if not all, of the following outcomes: cleaner air; a reduction in heat-island effect in urban areas; a moderation in the impact of climate change; increased energy efficiency; and the protection of source water.

Having an ecoinfrastructure in the masterplan is vital to any ecomasterplanning endeavour. Without it, no matter how clever or advanced is the eco-engineering gadgetry used, the masterplan remains simply a work of engineering, and can in no way be called an ecological masterplan nor, in the case of larger developments, an eco-city.

These linear wildlife corridors connect existing green spaces and large areas, and can create new, larger habitats in their own right, or may be in the form of newly linked existing woodland belts or wetlands, or existing landscape features, such as overgrown railway lines, hedges and waterways. Any new green infrastructure must clearly also complement and enhance the natural functions of what is already there in the landscape.

During the initial context study in the masterplanning process, the designer identifies existing green routes and green areas, and possible new routes and linkages for creating new connections in the landscape. It is at this point that additional green functional landscape elements or zones can also be integrated, such as linking to existing waterways that also provide ecological services, such as drainage to attenuate flooding.

In the masterplan, this ecoinfrastructure should serve as the dominant green infrastructure in the landscape, as the natural infrastructure, and should take precedence over other engineering infrastructures in the masterplan. By creating, improving and rehabilitating ecological connectivity of the immediate environment, the ecoinfrastructure turns human intervention in the landscape from a negative into a positive. Its environmental benefits and values are an armature and framework for natural systems and functions that are ecologically fundamental to the viability of the locality's plant and animal species and their habitat, such as healthy soils, water and air. It reverses the fragmentation of natural habitats and encourages increases in biodiversity to restore functioning ecosystems while providing the fabric for sustainable living, and safeguarding and enhancing natural features.

This new connectivity of the landscape with the built form is both a horizontal and a vertical endeavour. An obvious demonstration of horizontal connectivity is the provision of ecological corridors and links in regional and local planning that are crucial for making urban patterns more biologically viable. Connectivity over impervious surfaces and roads can be achieved by using ecological bridges, undercrofts and ramps. Besides improved horizontal connectivity, vertical connectivity with human buildings is also necessary since most buildings are not single storey but multistorey. Design must extend the ecological corridors vertically upwards, with greenery spanning a building – from the foundations to the green gardens on the roof tops.

Supporting existing practices in sustainable resource management, the ecoinfrastructure provides a structure and strategy for sustainable management of land and water resources, such as the production of energy, growth of food crops, pollution control, climatic amelioration and increased porosity of land cover. It is vital to biodiversity, particularly relating to the importance of the connectivity of habitats at a variety of landscape scales. It enables new urban developments to offset climate-change effects, with vegetation acting effectively as an ecological service-provider, balancing and modifying negative impacts

Ecoinfrastructure as an Ecological Service-Provider, Offsetting Climate Change

- Carbon sinks: Trees have a significant capacity to absorb carbon dioxide. A single hectare (2.49 acres) of woodland can absorb CO_2 emissions equivalent to those from 100 family cars.
- Pollution control: Vegetation has a significant capacity to attenuate noise and filter air pollution from motor vehicles. Street trees can remove sulphur dioxide and reduce particulates by up to 75 per cent. Noise attenuation can be as much as 30 dB per 100 metres (328 feet). Wetland ecosystems are also effective in filtering polluted runoff and sewage.
- Natural cooling: In urban areas the heat-island effect can increase temperatures by 5°C (9°F) compared to those of adjacent open countryside. Vegetation provides natural air conditioning. A single large tree can produce a cooling effect similar to air conditioning five rooms and will supply enough oxygen for 10 people.
- Microclimate control: Vegetation can improve microclimate conditions by providing shade in summer. It can also reduce wind effects created by streets, and wind loads on buildings, potentially reducing heating requirements by up to 25 per cent.
- Flood prevention: Vegetation can reduce excessive runoff and increase rainfall capture. This reduces the risk of flooding in low-lying areas and can also recharge soil moisture and groundwater.

Ecoinfrastructure with green ramps.

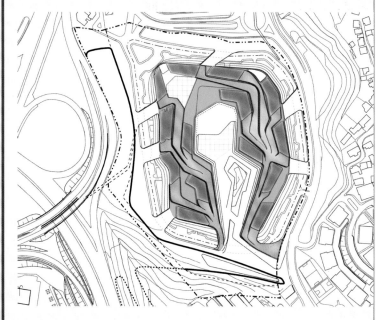

Horizontal and vertical integration.

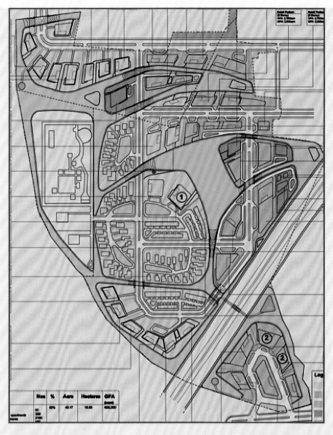

**Llewellyn Davies Yeang and TR Hamzah & Yeang
Sdn Bhd, SOMA Masterplan, Bangalore, India, 2008**
Ecomasterplan.

Ecomasterplanning as the weaving of four
infrastructures: the green ecoinfrastructure (nature's
infrastructure); the blue infrastructure (the sustainable
drainage and surface-water management
infrastructure); the grey infrastructure (roads,
sewerage, IT and other sustainable eco-engineering
systems); and the human infrastructure (built systems,
hardscapes, human regulatory systems, and so on).

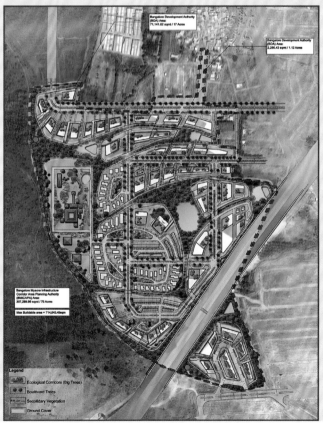

on the environment such as carbon-dioxide emissions and heat-island effect in urban areas (see box).

The green infrastructure network can be used to define the hierarchy and form of the habitats and natural green spaces within a community. The opportunities will be defined by the scale and form of the masterplan and its associated infrastructure.

The network will need to integrate and establish links with ecologically valuable elements of the existing green infrastructure, and resolve the functional requirements of urban form, such as green-space provision, habitat networks and ecological services like drainage.

In this way, ecoinfrastructure provides the strategic connection of open green areas. It forms the physical green environment within and between our built environment (cities, towns and villages) as a network of multifunctional open spaces (including formal parks, gardens, woodlands, green corridors, waterways, street trees and open countryside). In the masterplan it can also relate to the planning of recreational facilities and spaces, particularly relating to the use of non-car routes to address public health and quality-of-life issues. The ecoinfrastructure comprises all environmental resources, contributing towards sustainable resource management.

The Grey Infrastructure
The grey infrastructure is the usual urban engineering infrastructure such as roads, drains, sewerage, water reticulation, telecommunications, and energy and electric power distribution systems. These engineering systems should integrate with the green infrastructure rather than vice versa, and should be designed as sustainable engineering systems.

The Blue Infrastructure
Parallel to the ecological infrastructure is the surface water infrastructure (the blue infrastructure) where the surface water from rain is retained within the site and is returned to the land for the recharging of groundwater by means of filtration beds, pervious roadways and built surfaces, retention ponds and bio-swales.

Ecomasterplanning must take into consideration the site's natural drainage patterns and provide surface-water management so that the rainfall remains within the locality and is not drained away into water bodies. Combined with the ecoinfrastructure, storm-water management enables the natural processes to infiltrate, evapo-transpire, or capture and use storm-water on or near the site where it falls while potentially generating other environmental benefits.

Wetland greenways are waterways with associated wetland and woodland habitats. Waterways should not be culverted or be deculverting of engineered waterways, but should be replaced with the introduction of wetlands and buffer strips of ecologically functional meadow and woodland habitats. Sealed surfaces can reduce soil moisture and leave low-lying areas susceptible to flooding from excessive runoff. Wetland greenways need to be designed as sustainable drainage systems to provide ecological services. Buffer can be integrated with linear green spaces to maximise their habitat potential.

Ecomasterplanning must create sustainable urban drainage systems that can function as wetland habitats. This is not only to alleviate flooding, but also to create buffer strips for habitat creation. While the width of the buffer strips may be constrained by existing land uses, their integration through linear green spaces can allow for wider corridors. Surface-water management maximises habitat potential. Intermittent waterway tributaries can be linked up using swales. Contaminants, for example from surface car-parking, may need pretreatment by reed beds. Tree planting may be required for bank protection and sediment may require periodic removal.

The Red (or Human) Infrastructure
The human infrastructure is the human community, its built environment (buildings, houses etc), hardscapes and regulatory systems (laws, regulations, ethics, etc).

Ecomasterplanning Versus Conventional Masterplanning
What differentiates ecomasterplanning from conventional masterplanning is the green infrastructure. The provision of the green infrastructure differs from conventional open-space planning because it considers multiple functions and benefits of ecosystems and green space in concert with land development, sustainable resource management and built infrastructure planning. It can also be applied and integrated at both the macro- and micro- scales.

Green infrastructure planning also works at national, regional and local levels. At the regional level, for instance, the ecoinfrastructure becomes the network of functional seminatural, natural and artificial environments, and open spaces within and between cities, towns and villages. It is set within, and is a part of, a high-quality natural and built environment, delivering many of the social, economic and environmental benefits required for sustainable communities. At a national scale, green infrastructure can work as an integral component to planning well-designed and sustainable communities across entire regions. Δ+

Ken Yeang is a director of Llewelyn Davies Yeang in London and TR Hamzah & Yeang, its sister company, in Kuala Lumpur, Malaysia. He is the author of many articles and books on sustainable design, including *Ecodesign: A Manual for Ecological Design* (Wiley-Academy 2006).

Drawing Strength From Machinery

In a paean to the mechanistic, Neil Spiller draws our attention to how Bryan Cantley of FORM:uLA in Los Angeles is a creating a little-known 'laboratory of form casting four-dimensional cartographies for possible new architectures'.

Twenty years ago, Princeton Architectural Press published the very successful 'Building Machines' issue of *Pamphlet Architecture*. It featured the mechanistic visions of Pfau/Jones, Neil Denari and the gorgeously Dada works of Kaplan and Krueger. Real machines for living in inspired by hydraulic lines, JCBs, fork-lift trucks, aircraft and all the metallic paraphernalia of late 20th-century existence just before the computer became ubiquitous. It became an important bench mark in the 'Architecture as Machine' idiom.

That was then and now is now – all things return but differently. Over the last 15 years, Los Angeles teacher and practitioner Bryan Cantley has added to this

particular genealogy of architecture and has produced a substantial body of work, which should be much better known than it is. Cantley's work with his practice Form:uLA is forward thinking while obviously referencing the seminal work done before. But it is designed for a different world. A world where the computer reigns supreme, and where machines and virtual machines are forever changing guises and functions.

Contemporary existence involves navigating and operating a gamut of differing technologies and being conversant with a whole number of operational protocols. Imagine sitting on an aeroplane, while watching a video, with a telephone in the armrest, an asthma inhaler in the pocket, a razor in the luggage and a Valentine's card rubbing against your laptop in its snug little bag. These simple everyday scenarios are

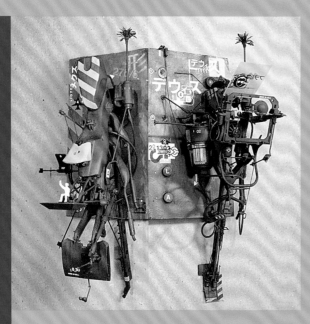

Models are made quickly from found objects, model kits and the compositional expediency that a time-limited concoction affords. Graphic hieroglyphics and semiotics are just as important as the formal qualities of each design. Model by Bryan Cantley and Kevin O'Donnell.

Programatically, though not truly a simultaneous event, the Mobile Gatherspace (Hovering Cityscape) was explored as an entity that would travel from location to location, position to position, encountering various site and contextual conditions, becoming a floating civic plaza and lightly programmed support spaces that would never have a single, given 'place'. It would travel where needed, and leave as soon as the immediate need was quenched.

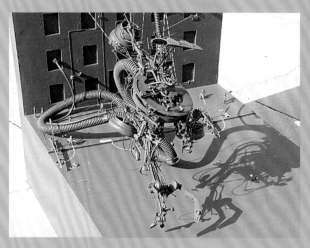

The Seedplanter is attached to a given generic architectural condition. It gathers data from the context; from the street; from the surrounding area; from inhabitants and passers-by, and plugs the information back into itself. After processing occurs, 'epigenetic pods' are planted/embedded on the site to develop into programmable architectural parasites. These may become inhabited spaces, service components or facade 'corrections'/augmentations, as the need arises.

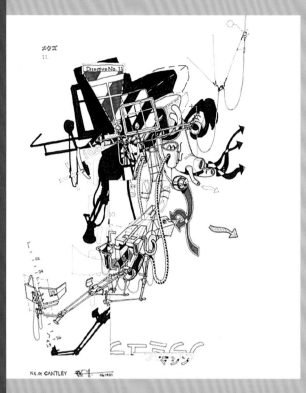

Form:uLA's drawing and sketching style is clear and unambiguous, yet still affords space for reinterpretation.

the conceptual sites for FORM:uLA's architecture, which surfs, records and posits in these fluxing machinic topologies and typologies. The real sites are often the interstitial spaces of the contemporary city, its facades and its datums. In turn FORM:uLA's assemblies have a spatial fecundity of their own – that cossets and breeds spaces in tune with need, desire and expediency. They are urban implants that mesh into roofscapes, sidewalks and window reveals – forcing space and regenerating it.

A FORM:uLA piece is a laboratory of form casting four-dimensional cartographies for possible new architectures. Formally the work has a kind of alien presence similar to a salon hairdryer out of control or behind the dashboard of a car or a mutant Airfix kit (an F111 meets Lawrence of Arabia's motorbike while on a trip to Japan). Similar to Neil Denari, whose father worked in aerospace, Cantley grew up on an American farm playing on tractors and other large farm machinery and experiencing a landscape calibrated by these metallic leviathans. Indeed, the pieces themselves still often retain the scale of the combine harvester. Yet they also resonate with the notion of the 'combine' in the art of Robert Rauschenberg – an architecture of ready-made mass-produced objects,

transferred images, subverted iconography and emphasis on the viewer completing the work.

As FORM:uLA explain, their architecture has the 'potential to exist in many places, or rather ANY place, at any given time. It is both site-less, and of many-sites. It lies somewhere between the idea of mobility and multi-spatiality. Since the fabric of public open space often defines the urban setting, we saw this as an opportunity to allow critical need to determine architectural experimentation. Thus the idea of a docking station or site-specific system requirement at each site was also considered in the design of the project. We have been asked numerous times "where the lines go that thrust off the edge of the page". This "docking scenario", or the notion of a place download, is one answer.'

FORM:uLA and Bryan Cantley intrigue me, I should have seen this work earlier and so should have you. Go on, give Bryan Cantley a Google – you will be amazed. You have not seen the last of this practice. **Δ+**

Neil Spiller is Professor of Architecture and Digital Theory and Vice Dean at the Bartlett School of Architecture, University College London.

MᴄLᴇᴀɴ's Nᴜɢɢᴇᴛs

Fractals

When each piece of a shape is geometrically similar to the whole, both the shape and the cascade that generate it are called self-similar.
–BB Mandelbrot, *The Fractal Geometry of Nature*, 1982[1]

For newcomers to the field of fractals and fractal geometry, we may introduce the fractal as a term to describe self-similarity. Useful examples in the natural world include the fern, which if you remove a stem looks remarkably 'similar' to the leaf from which it was removed, or the more edible broccoli and cauliflower, which exhibit at least three scales of 'similar' morphology – break off a broccoli floret and you have a broccoli in miniature, etc. Another well-used example is the profile of a coastline, which when studied in plan through aerial photography or mapping exhibits a similar geometric profile at a range of scales. You may zoom in to pick up more detail and definition, but the underlying shapes are the same: the world displaying a degree of what Mandelbrot called 'regular irregularity'. This technique of jumping scales was usefully illustrated in Charles and Ray Eames' film *Powers of Ten* made for IBM in 1977, where through the starting point of an aerially observed picnic, we zoom back to the outer reaches of the cosmos and then zoom in to the smallest observable (or imaginable) molecular structure, with the two extremes bearing an uncanny resemblance, which may not be physically exact but is pedagogically neat.

In the mind's eye, a fractal is a way of seeing infinity.
–James Gleick, *Chaos: Making a New Science*, 1987[2]

Fractals are like worlds within worlds, whose visual psychedelic potential was unleashed only through the iterative possibility of the computer. Rumour has it that some Mandelbrot mathematics were left churning on some CPU, which when returned to had produced some hitherto unimaginable complex graphic noodlings of paisleyesque complexity. A new variant of these scalar transformations recently spotted was the Klassnik Corporation's High Profile Tower SFK70 x 154.29. The extruded profile of an SFK70 aluminium window system generates the interior complexity for a mixed-use tower when multiplied in scale by a factor of 154.29. To create an inhabitable, climatically controlled structure, extrusion windows within the tower are fitted with the same SFK70 system. Tomas Klassnik (www.klassnik.com) meanwhile eschews his self-imposed corporate identity to produce an intriguing range of architectural propositions and ideas at a range of social and economic scales.

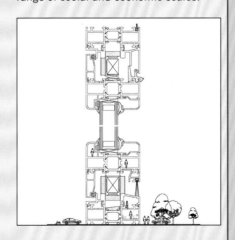

Klassnik Corporation's High Profile Tower SFK70 x 154.29.

Heterotopic Tower

Engaging with Michel Foucault's call for *espaces autres* (other spaces), architect Adam Kalkin has often referred to the notion of heterotopic spaces, or heterotopias, in his architecture. In this instance a commission from Yahoo creates a wi-fi tower with a series of miniature vertically stacked rooms. Accessed from an external steel stairway, which winds up and around the up-ended shipping containers, an instant skyscraper is created. Each floor is a totally separate installation that people can visit. It is designed primarily for college campuses. One floor is a hot tub for students to use, the top floor is a radio studio programmed by the Black Panthers, one floor sells Yahoo products, and on another is a psychotherapist taking patients. The tower stays for two or three days then travels to another college. It goes up in three hours and is anchored to the ground with helical screw piles.

Yahoo Heterotopic Tower designed by Adam Kalkin, 2008. Render by Keiko Mano.

Jean Dubuffet, *Garden of Enamel*, Kröller-Müller Museum, The Netherlands.

Positively No

I would like to make the case for the positive no. This is not the reactionary postulation of the sceptic or ideologically atrophied, but a demonstrably positive act of dissonance, where the 'spoilt' ballot paper is no longer an act of vandalism, stupidity or clerical error, but a thoughtful and expedient response to a political circumstance.

Orthodoxy is not always optimised behaviour and can engender intellectual laziness and cowardice. If art has a role in the world, it is to confront one's prejudices and learnt stasis. Incidentally, this may also be a hugely enjoyable process and produce some interesting artefacts along the way. Jean Dubuffet's 'Art Brut' was to question the learned assumptions of so-called culture with the neo-primitive tools of a rough-cut, lumpy art and invective:

The time is right to found institutes of deculturation, kinds of nihilist gymnasiums … who would keep protestation alive, at least in small, isolated and exceptional circles, in the midst of the great and widespread waves of cultural accord.
Jean Dubuffet, *Asphyxiating Culture and Other Writings*, 1988[3]

This kind of single-mindedness produced some monochrome works of great beauty, in particular his *Garden of Enamel* at the Kröller-Müller Museum in the Netherlands, where a black-and-white elevated landscape is accessed through a hole in a wall. Having entered you are guided up a small winding stair fashioned from a single surface, and emerge from a tree-like object on to a roughly undulating surface of steps and pools. This 'otherworldly' place was once said to have hosted a lecture by engineering polymath Frei Otto and the sartorially monochrome Cedric Price.

Anyhow, back to being negative (or was that questioning assumptions?). At a recent Performing Arts Labs (PAL; www.pallabs.org) event in Kent, Stem Fluency Lab tested the new STEM (Science, Technology, Engineering and Mathematics) curriculum for the Nuffield Curriculum Centre. Through the thematic conceit of the No-lympics[4] (an ad-hoc event to be designed and hosted by students), all basic assumptions about an olympiad were questioned to produce a series of newly formatted events that test and investigate the mental and physical limits of the individual against the backdrop of his or her own physical environment, and not that of the highly prescribed sports orthodoxy. What emerged out of this 'negative' approach was a set of self-organising events launched with a no-national anthem, which included phenomenological sports such as shadow boxing and a Fibonacci podium, on which stood no winners, just participants of an elegant arithmetic progression. ∆+

'McLean's Nuggets' is an ongoing technical series inspired by Will McLean and Samantha Hardingham's enthusiasm for back issues of *AD*, as explicitly explored in Hardingham's *AD* issue *The 1970s is Here and Now* (March/April 2005).

Will McLean is joint coordinator of Technical Studies at the University of Westminster's School of Architecture. October 2008 will see the launch of *Introduction to Architectural Technology* co-authored with Pete Silver and published by Laurence King. McLean has recently launched his own imprint, Bibliotheque McLean, and has recently published *Quik Build: An Open Source Book For Container Architecture* about the work of US architect Adam Kalkin.

Notes

1. BB Mandelbrot, *The Fractal Geometry of Nature*, WH Freeman & Co (New York), 1982.
2. James Gleick, *Chaos: Making a New Science*, Penguin (London), 1987.
3. Jean Dubuffet, *Asphyxiating Culture and Other Writings*, trans Carol Volk, Four Walls Eight Windows (New York), 1988.
4. 'No-lympics (The ad-hoc olympiad)' was devised by Cathy Bereznicki, Simon Hall, Matt Lambourne, William McLean and Jenny Wales and took place at PAL, Stem Fluency Lab, Bore Place, Kent, 20–25 April 2008.

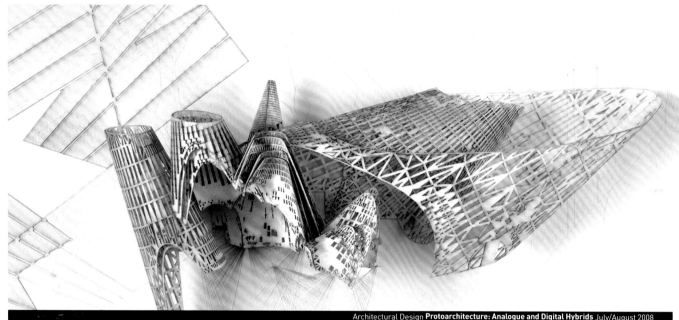

What is Architectural Design?

Launched in 1930, *Architectural Design* is an influential and prestigious architectural publication. With an almost unrivalled reputation worldwide, it is consistently at the forefront of cultural thought and design.

Architectural Design is published bimonthly. Features include:

Main section
The main section of every issue functions as a book and is guest-edited by a leading international expert in the field.

△+
The △+ magazine section at the back of every issue includes ongoing series and regular columns.

Truly international in terms of the subjects covered and its contributors, *Architectural Design*:

- focuses on cutting-edge design
- combines the currency and topicality of a newsstand journal with the rigour and production qualities of a book
- is provocative and inspirational, inspiring theoretical, creative and technological advances
- questions the outcomes of technical innovations as well as the far-reaching social, cultural and environmental challenges that present themselves today

How to Subscribe

With 6 issues a year, you can subscribe to △ (either print or online), or buy titles individually.

Subscribe today to receive 6 issues delivered direct to your door!

£198 / US$369	institutional subscription (combined print and online)
£180 / US$335	institutional subscription (print or online)
£110 / US$170	personal rate subscription (print only)
£70 / US$110	student rate subscription (print only)
To subscribe:	Tel: +44 (0) 843 828
	Email: cs-journals@wiley.com

To purchase individual titles go to:
www.wiley.com

Made in India, guest-edited by Kazi K Ashraf, is the recipient of the Pierre Vago Journalism Award 2008, awarded by the CICA International Book Awards